Foster's Histori...

CW00384722

The Author

Allen Foster lives on a farm in Enfield, Co. Meath. When not tending to his cattle or walking his beloved dogs, he finds the time to be a freelance journalist and researcher. He is the author of eight other books, including *Foster's Irish Oddities, Foster's Even Odder Irish Oddities* and *Around the World with Citizen Train: The Sensational Adventures of the Real Phileas Fogg.*

Historical Irish
Oddities

A Compendium of Extraordinary But True Tales

Allen Foster

Gill Books

Gill Books
Hume Avenue
Park West
Dublin 12
www.gillbooks.ie

Gill Books is an imprint of M.H. Gill and Co.

Previously published in hardback as *Foster's Historical Irish Oddities*, 2015

978 07171 8472 9

Design and print origination by O'K Graphic Design, Dublin
Illustrations by Douglas Ferris
Printed and bound by ScandBook AB, Sweden

This book is typeset in 11/15 pt Minion.

The paper used in this book comes from the wood pulp of managed forests. For every tree felled, at least one tree is planted, thereby renewing natural resources.

A CIP catalogue record for this book is available from the British Library.

5 4 3 2 1

Acknowledgements

Thanks to Jonathan Williams, Douglas Ferris and Michael Potterton for all their support over the course of writing this book.

Thanks also to all at Gill Books, particularly Deirdre Nolan, Ruth Mahony and Jane Rogers.

On the morning of 1 October 1941 a porter working on the North Wall Docks in Dublin upended a large case that had been accidentally turned upside down the night before when it was being unloaded from the ship *Slieve Bawn* from Liverpool. The porter thought it was his imagination when he heard tapping coming from inside the crate. He listened carefully and it started again. He tapped the case and received an answering tap from inside. He called other porters to help and the case was quickly opened.

The men were amazed to find a hysterical semi-conscious Frenchman upside down and encased in a large plaster cast. The frantic man was brought to Jervis Street hospital. There he identified himself as 40-year-old Maurice Carcassus de Laboujac, an artist with an address in London.

M. de Laboujac's paintings were due to go on show in Dublin, but he was unable to obtain the necessary visa, so he arranged to ship himself inside the crate to a Dublin art gallery on Molesworth Street. The Frenchman planned his trip carefully and had a plaster cast made which fitted his body and prevented him being buffeted too severely in the packing case. He spent four days en route from London to Dublin.

Everything had gone to plan until a careless dockworker unloaded the packing case and left it upside down with its occupant standing on his head and unable to do anything about it.

❧❧❧

Newspapers from January 1928 claimed that limpets in County Donegal had killed thousands of rats that winter. It was said that the armies of rats that infested the islands on the north-west coast off Donegal had been venturing to the shoreline in search of food. At low tide, the rats inserted their noses into the partly open shells of the limpets, hoping to make a meal of the edible shellfish, but the limpet is very sensitive to touch and instantly closed on the rats with a vice-like grip. The rats were held tight until the rising tide crept in and drowned them.

❧❧❧

At the age of 97 in the early 1820s, Mr Huddy, the postmaster of Lismore, County Waterford bet a friend that he would ride from that town to Fermoy in a Dungarvan oyster tub, pulled by a pig, a badger, two cats, a goose and a hedgehog. Huddy would wear a large red nightcap and urge his motley team on with a pig-driver's whip and cow horn.

According to a newspaper report on 8 January 1821, a large number of spectators gathered to witness him perform this extraordinary feat and Huddy completed his epic journey and collected his winnings.

❧❧❧

Mary O'Brien (*c.* 1721–1791) was the eldest daughter of Lady Orkney and Lord Inchiquin, and became 3rd Countess of Orkney in her own right in 1766 when her mother died without a male heir. She was deaf and dumb and in 1753 was married, by signing, to her first cousin, Murrough O'Brien, 1st Marquess of Thomond. They lived in Rostellan, County Cork. Shortly after the birth of their first child, a nurse saw the Countess quietly approach the child's cot. The nurse looked on in horror as the Countess raised a big stone over her sleeping child, then threw it to the ground. As the stone hit the floor, the child awoke and cried out. The Countess was delighted, now that she was certain that her infant was not deaf or dumb like her.

❧❧❧

Among the most notorious mayors of Limerick city was Edmund Sexton (1486–1555), a renegade Irishman who enjoyed the patronage of King Henry VIII and was granted much forfeited land after the dissolution of the monasteries. He also defeated fellow Irishmen on several occasions in battles and sieges and claimed to have prevented the destruction of the city of Limerick by Lord Leonard Grey, the Lord Deputy. After his death, he was buried in St Mary's Cathedral. Sometime later his corpse was stolen from his tomb and hung by its heels from the roof where it remained undiscovered for three years.

❧❧❧

A remarkable case of sleepwalking was reported to have occurred in Tramore, County Waterford in September 1885. A young man, a tourist, took a room for the night in the Railway Hotel and went to bed. About three o'clock in the morning some stragglers saw a man, in his nightclothes and holding a lighted candle, raise a window on the second floor of the hotel and lower himself from it, before falling another fifteen feet to the ground. The fall did not affect the man, and with the lighted candle still in his hand he walked into the town and knocked on a door.

Now he woke up and wondered where he was. The owners of the house at which he had knocked kindly lent him shoes, a hat and an old coat and brought him to the police barracks to get help. Seeing the distressed state the man was in, the sergeant provided him with food and clothes. The policeman made enquires at the hotel and found the man's luggage, including a gold watch and over £15 in cash. It is safe to say that it was one holiday the sleepwalking tourist would remember.

❧❧❧

According to the March 1769 *Annual Register*, a party of gentleman were hunting near Lough Tay in Wicklow when a large eagle swooped down, seized their terrier and flew off. Fearful of hitting the dog if they shot at the eagle, the men could only stand and watch as the bird of prey carried away its victim. They shouted to encourage the dog to attack its captor, not that the terrier needed to be told what to do. It put up a fierce struggle and managed to grab a wing with its jaws and bring down the eagle. The bird was flying low at the time, so the dog was not injured in the fall and held on tightly to its would-be captor until the men secured the eagle. It measured seven feet from wing tip to wing tip and the article says that the hunters planned to give it as a present to the Marquess of Waterford.

❧❧❧

A strange tale from Waterford featured in newspapers in July 1904. A beautiful and very popular young woman died and was buried in a cemetery in the county. Early next morning a farmer living nearby rose to go about his work. Hearing a noise, he looked over the graveyard wall and was astonished to see a stranger on his knees beside the newly filled-in grave. The man was frantically digging at the grave with his hands. When the coffin was uncovered, the man wrenched off its lid with an iron bar. Bending over the corpse, the man gazed for a while at the face of the dead girl, kissed her forehead, then replaced the lid and refilled the grave. Alerted by the farmer, the police arrived and arrested the stranger.

In the man's pocket was a telegram sent from Waterford to him in Bristol telling him of the young lady's death. After reading this news, the man rushed back to Waterford for a final reunion. When arrested, he said, 'They thought they could prevent me seeing her, but they were mistaken.' He was taken before a magistrate, who committed him to a mental asylum.

❧❦❧

There appear to be only two accounts in medical literature concerning sudden loss of hair. In the *Report of the British Association*, 1843, a Dr O'Connor describes the case of a 12-year-old boy whose hair, eyebrows and eyelashes suddenly fell off after the boy had a fright. Daniel McCarthy, a farmer's son from near Kinsale, County Cork was in good health.

One night he woke up screaming and frightened his family. He told them he had dreamed that two men were dragging him from the house to murder him. The next day his hair began to fall out. Inside a fortnight he was completely bald and not a hair remained on his eyebrows or eyelashes. Seven years later he still had no hair, but was otherwise in good health.

❧❧❧

Nicholas Arthur (1405–1465) was mayor of Limerick seven times and was also the father of four successive mayors of Limerick.

❧❧❧

A curious treasure trove was unearthed in two houses in Belfast in April 1901 at an estate auction held after the death of two elderly sisters. The women had kept themselves to themselves, and neighbours were under the impression that they were badly off, frequently bringing them food.

The auction of the two houses and their contents got off to a poor start. The auctioneer managed to raise a bid of only one pound for a decrepit piano when an old lady sat down at the stool and began to pass her fingers over the keyboard. She took down a front panel, found a bulky bag inside and opened it. The bag was full of money – several hundred pounds – which she handed to the auctioneer. No other hidden valuables were found, so the auction continued.

Since the sisters had died without making a will, the entire estate fell to the Irish government, and two policemen were present to ensure that proceedings went smoothly. One bulky police constable fell through a ground floor into another room when the floorboards gave way. The bidders became uneasy about their safety, so the auctioneer called a carpenter and had the floor repaired. After raising one of the floorboards, he discovered several hundred pounds in rolls of banknotes and gave these to the auctioneer.

After this second discovery, bidding was brisk for any unsold contents and for the houses themselves.

❧❦❧

Lightning that struck a house near Ballyglass, County Mayo on 5 January 1890 had a peculiar effect on a basket of eggs lying on the floor of one of the rooms. The shells were shattered so that they fell off when the eggs were put in boiling water, but the inner membrane was not broken. The house owner boiled a few eggs from the top of the basket and they tasted fine. Remarkably, those at the bottom of the basket were flattened, but not broken.

❧❦❧

By 1884 cockfighting had been banned in Ireland for some years and almost completely stamped out, but lovers of the cruel sport endeavoured to stage contests and evade the law.

On 27 June 1884 promoters ensured that they would not be disturbed by police, or be betrayed, by staging a contest on board a steamer in Dublin Bay which they had hired especially for the purpose. For some time, teams from the north of Ireland and Liverpool had planned to hold a contest for prize money of £200 in Dublin and they arrived in the city on 26 June to carry out their plan. The organisers were worried that police would find and raid any premises where they held the cockfighting and decided to use a novel venue. That night, word was sent round to all contestants and onlookers to gather at a hotel at the North Wall the following morning.

Once all fifty or sixty men had arrived, they were quickly ushered on board the chartered steamer, whose captain and crew were ignorant of what was going on until the birds were brought on board. The boat steamed out into Dublin Bay and the anchored was dropped. The afterdeck was carpeted and transformed into a pit for the brutal contest. A referee was appointed and five battles were staged. A vast sum of money was gambled on the outcome of each. The contests started at 11 a.m. and went on until 3 p.m., when the steamer returned to Dublin. The Irish birds were victorious.

❧❧❧

The great oak of Portmore stood on the grounds of Portmore Castle near Lisburn, County Antrim. This magnificent tree made a small fortune for its owner when it blew down in 1760. Its circumference was 42 feet, and from the lowest branch to the ground was 25 feet. A branch made £9 and the trunk sold for £97. Part of the remainder was used to build a ship of forty tons' burden.

❧❧❧

Frank Dwyer from Cashel, County Tipperary was a well-liked eccentric known to all as 'Franky Doodle'. When his landlord, Daniel Kyte, died in 1888, Dwyer refused to pay any further rent, claiming that Kyte had left him the house (along with a coffin, which Dwyer kept in his bedroom). The law saw differently and an eviction notice was issued. When, on 5 July 1888, the bailiffs arrived at the house on William Street to evict Dwyer, they discovered that he had locked the doors and securely barricaded himself inside. Franky stuck his head out of one of the upstairs windows and shouted, 'You can't evict me out of the coffin, and you must put me out, coffin and all.'

After some discussion, Dwyer agreed to surrender the house, but only on condition that he was evicted while lying in his coffin. The bailiffs agreed to Dwyer's curious terms and removed the barricades, after which he threw down the key. When the bailiffs and police gained entry, they found Dwyer upstairs in the bedroom lying serenely in the coffin, waiting. Because the stairs were so narrow, they had to lower the coffin and its occupant out through one of the windows. Many townspeople gathered to watch the bailiffs and police lowering the unpainted open coffin with Franky reclining in it.

Dwyer reportedly wore a 'high silk hat, around which was twined an old white veil'. As they lowered him to the ground, Franky loudly protested to the crowd about his 'illegal eviction'. The spectators enjoyed the show immensely. As a fitting finale, some youths picked up the coffin, put it on their shoulders and marched up the Main Street with Franky sitting upright in it, followed by a large crowd cheering their local hero.

T.P. Flanagan and J.P. McCormack from Castlebar, County Mayo were fishing on Lough Mask in October 1935 when there was a heavy downpour. The men sheltered on the larger of two islands near the Cushlough side of the lake. When the rain stopped, the anglers were pushing off from the island in their boat when they heard the terrified shrieks of an animal coming from the smaller island. They turned the boat around and saw an adult hare being chased by a weasel.

As they watched in horror, the hare jumped into the water and swam towards the other island some twenty yards away, closely pursued by the weasel. Flanagan and McCormack reached the island after the hare and weasel had landed. The exhausted hare heard them come ashore, ran towards the men and jumped into McCormack's arms. The weasel was still in hot pursuit of its prey, but McCormack, holding the hare carefully, managed to fire off a shot at the weasel, which escaped into the long grass unharmed. Undeterred by being shot at, the weasel followed the men, but McCormack fired again and killed it. They then released the hare.

Garda Michael Burke from Ahascragh, County Galway had an inch-long needle removed from his arm at the Central Hospital in Galway in February 1927. He did not remember how the needle had entered his body and thought he must have swallowed it when he was a child.

❧❧

During a storm off the coast of Galway on 7 March 1840, the British Revenue cruiser HMS *Chichester*, commanded by Captain Stuart, was badly damaged by ball lightning that descended from the mainmast and broke through the deck, knocking down several crew members as it did so. It passed through the captain's cabin while he and his two daughters were eating dinner and floated over the table, shattering glasses and dishes.

Luckily no one was hurt, but the entire deck in the centre of the ship was raised off the beams, and the skylights were thrown up. All the patent lights were extinguished. The lightning passed through the bottom of the vessel along the copper bolts and tore off the copper sheathing opposite them on the hull. The ship's magnetic compasses no longer worked and the watches of those on board stopped. The *Chichester* was filled with smoke for some time after she was hit, and it was feared she was on fire. Thankfully this was not the case. By strengthening the mast, Captain Stuart was able to limp the ship safely to Greenock for repair.

❧❧

Jockey Mick Morrissey from Fethard, County Tipperary changed horses in mid-race at Southwell Race Course, Nottinghamshire on 15 October 1953 without ever touching the ground. He left the starting gate in the Upton Novices Steeplechase aboard Knother, a twenty to one shot. He crossed the finishing line last – on Royal Student, the favourite. It happened like this: Royal Student fell at the fifth fence, throwing its rider, Tim Molony from Croom, County Limerick. Knother crashed into Royal Student, tossing Morrissey high into the air. He came down just as Royal Student struggled to his feet – and landed in the saddle! Weary horse and rider finished the two-mile course at a walk.

❧❧

Duncan C. Parker, known as 'The Hermit of Kilmashogue', was a picturesque figure with a long black beard, who lived in an extraordinary house. Tired of his conventional life as a successful businessman in Dublin, he sold up and retired in 1911, then bought part of Kilmashogue mountain in south Dublin and built his strange house. Parker believed that a person's personality and character were determined by the direction of light that fell on them. The eccentric hermit held that it was important to get as much sunlight as possible, even to the point of positioning your bed so that it was directly in the sun's rays when it rose in the morning. Sleeping in a north-facing room, where the lack of direct sunlight allowed 'injurious microbes' to flourish, was highly dangerous.

The other points of the compass also had disadvantages; if you lived in a room facing east, you acquired energy, coupled, however, with a hard, material outlook; if your windows looked south, you were likely to become indolent; if you spent too much time facing the western sun, you were more likely to develop an artistic temperament.

Parker solved these difficulties by building a round house with windows facing every direction. Four roof windows faced the four points of the compass. The other seven were evenly spread around the house's granite walls. The roof was domed and made of three-ply wood. The hermit had two Primus stoves for heating and cooking and got water from a neighbouring stream. He lived happily in his remote abode until September 1920.

❧❦❧

Biddy Cassells (1835–1908) from Lisnageer, County Cavan hatched a hundred chickens by sitting on a nest of eggs for three weeks. When she was 67 years old, she disappeared one spring and was absent for three weeks. At the end of that time, Biddy came out of her hen house trailed by 100 baby chicks. She claimed to have hatched them by sitting on some of the eggs and covering the rest with the folds of her dress.

❧❦❧

The first Irish cat to emigrate to America belonged to Mary O'Sullivan from Ballybunion, County Kerry. Mrs O'Sullivan moved across the Atlantic to be with her children as she was getting old and there was no one left in Ballybunion to look after in her twilight years. She hated to leave her home, but in particular could not bear to leave behind her pet kitten. A bag and her beloved tabby cat were all the possessions Mrs O'Sullivan brought with her in 1898 to start a new life.

Patrick McManus and Henry Moore from Bantry Bay, County Cork last saw each other in 1877 before they both emigrated to different corners of the world. Moore sailed for New York and McManus for Liverpool. In the spring of 1907, eagle-eyed Moore was walking on Seventh Avenue in New York when he spotted Patrick McManus walking the opposite way on the other side of the street. Moore could not make his voice carry across the street noises or attract his friend's attention.

In his haste to reach McManus, Moore ran across the road and did not see a fast-approaching vehicle. He was knocked down and injured. Moore was more concerned about losing McManus than his own health and asked bystanders to catch his friend. After calling for an ambulance, a policeman raced after McManus and finally tracked him down some distance away. Moore had been loaded into an ambulance when McManus returned and was delighted to see his friend.

❦❦❦

Returning from a day's hunting at Newtown Cunningham in the autumn of 1838, a member of the Derry hunt riding a black horse named Rectifier, owned by one John Allen, won a wager by leaping over a cow standing in a field.

❦❦❦

Eighteen-year-old William Mooney was married to the widow Vincent, who was 105 years old, in Sligo in August 1772. This merry widow was first married in 1681 – ninety-one years before.

❦❦❦

Lady Arabella Denny presented a remarkable clock to the nursery of the Foundling Hospital in Dublin in 1760. An inscription on it read: 'For the benefit of infants protected by this hospital, Lady Arabella Denny presents this clock, to mark, that as children reared by the spoon must have but a small quantity of food at a time, it must be offered frequently; for which purpose, this clock strikes every 20 minutes, at which notice all the infants that are not asleep must be discreetly fed.'

❦❦

World War II caused unusual shortages in Ireland. Before the Emergency, the country imported several thousand frogs a year from England and Germany for research purposes in universities and hospitals. The supply dried up at the outset of the conflict and researchers had to find alternative supplies to keep going. The *Irish Times* of 4 October 1941 carried an article on the shortage with a dramatic headline that was sure to warm the heart of any small boy: 'Wanted – Frogs Fourpence Each'.

❦❦

Fishermen from the south-east of the country broke with long-established tradition by going to sea on an 'unlucky' day made a record catch on 11 November 1946. Driven to desperation by five weeks of inshore winds, which had left their boats tied up in port, the fishermen defied a tradition that had been followed for nearly two centuries. They put to sea on St Martin's night, which since the disaster of 11 November 1762, when seventy fishermen were drowned in a sudden storm in Rosslare Bay, has been considered unlucky. When the boats did not return on schedule, the families of the men from the Wexford towns of Courtown, Blackwater, Curracloe and Rosslare waited anxiously for news. Fortunately, the delay had been caused by a record catch and the fleet returned the following day with the best catch of the year.

❧❧

A Drogheda jarvey had a lucky escape on 30 January 1903 at the junction of Peter Street and Shop Street when his horse accidentally put its hind hoof in a hole in the road. When the horse and trap moved away, about three square yards of the street collapsed, leaving behind a twenty-foot hole. An examination showed that the subsidence had been caused when the large arched roof of an old disused sewer caved in. The streets were immediately closed off and workmen laboured night and day to fill in the hole.

❧❧

The *Downpatrick Recorder* of 15 May 1878 says: 'A marriage was celebrated in this neighbourhood during the present week in which the relationships of the parties were somewhat singular. It appears that the bridegroom's stepmother is his wife's sister; consequently the former is the mother of her own sister, and the bridegroom's wife is his own aunt. Should an heir arrive, the aunt of the heir will be his grandmother, and his grandfather will be his uncle. It will thus be seen that the connections between the parties are somewhat close and peculiar.'

❧❧

In the *British Medical Journal* of February 1951, Dr J.C. McMullin from County Cavan describes the strange story of one of his patients, a 24-year-old man, who was a 'human ostrich' and who had swallowed several strange objects. During an operation he was found to have almost the entire contents of a bicycle toolbag in his stomach. After the surgeon had removed a five-inch spanner, a three-inch tension spring, a 3½-inch steel twist drill, and a five-inch bicycle axle, the patient remarked some hours later: 'I am afraid there is a bit of a hacksaw yet.' The broken hacksaw was recovered by feeding the patient cotton-wool sandwiches. Dr McMullin says that the patient made an excellent recovery.

Andrew Newman from Robinstown near Mullingar, County Westmeath dug up a potato in November 1935 that weighed 2¾lb. On cutting it open, Newman found a pocket knife inside which he had lost two years before.

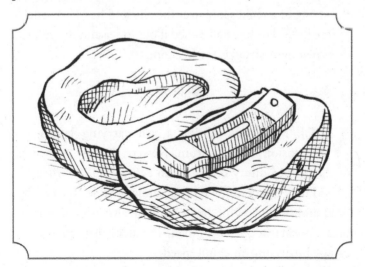

❧❧❧

Sir John Bellew (1520–1600) of Castletown, County Louth was married three times. He was his first wife's second husband, his second wife's fourth husband and his third wife's sixth husband.

❧❧❧

Fishermen out at sea near Belfast in August 1889 were puzzled by the sight of a large seagull floating on the water, fast approaching their boat, with wings outspread. It was clearly dead. They could not understand how the dead seagull could be moving faster than their boat. As they got near, the men saw that a string was wound fast around the bird's body and was attached to a large paper kite flying high over its head. The unfortunate bird had become entangled in the string of a child's kite over the city and had been unable to free itself. The kite had pulled it out to sea and the gull had drowned in its struggle for freedom.

❧❧❧

W.J. Boyle was driving a van carrying letters and pension money from Newry, County Down to Carlingford, County Louth on 26 February 1920 when five armed men attacked his vehicle a mile outside Newry. They fired and Boyle was hit, but a book he always carried in his breast pocket stopped the bullet. The lucky man managed to escape by driving on at full speed.

❧❦❧

While trying to clear beggars from The Loop, the historic centre of downtown Chicago, police arrested legless Irishman John Liston in July 1936. They discovered that he had $100 in his pockets and almost $48,000 in bank accounts. When asked to account for this hoard, the 65-year-old beggar explained that he had received $35,000 for losing his legs in a railway accident and had accumulated the rest of his fortune at the rate of $100 a month by selling pencils. The wealthy Irishman was held without charge pending a federal income tax inquiry. In November a court found Liston insane and sent him to Mereyville sanatorium at Aurora, Illinois. He was placed under the care of his sister, Mrs Helen Liston Hartnett, from New York. At his sanity trial, it was revealed that on his death his fortune would go to his sister and a brother back in Ireland, neither of whom had he seen for twenty years.

❧❦❧

The following curious notice appeared on the door of a church in the west of Ireland in 1820:

RUN AWAY FROM PATRICK McDALLAGH
Whereas my wife Mrs Bridget McDallagh, is again walked away with herself, and left me with four small children, and her poor blind mother, and nobody else to look after house and home, and, I hear, has taken up with Tim Guigan, the lame fiddler – the

same that was out in the stocks last Easter for stealing
Barday Doody's gamecock. This is to give notice, that
I will not pay for bite or sup on her or his account to
man or mortal, and that she had better never show
the mark of her ten toes near my home again.
PATRICK McDALLAGH
N.B. Tim had better keep out of my sight.

❧❧❧

Robert Macnish, in his 1836 book *The Philosophy of Sleep*,
recounts a story told to him by a doctor concerning an
Irish porter who was working in a London warehouse. The
Irishman would forget, when sober, what he had done when
he was drunk, but when drunk again would remember what
he had done when previously intoxicated. On one occasion
when he was drunk, he had lost a valuable parcel. No matter
how hard he tried to remember where he had left it, the sober
porter could not recall what he had done with it. The next
time he was drunk, he remembered he had left it at a certain
house. When he went to collect the parcel, it was waiting for
him.

❧❧❧

Robert Southey, in his 1812 book *Omniana*, mentions a
dog whose loyalty went beyond common sense. 'A dog
which had belonged to an Irishman, and was sold by him in
England, would never touch a morsel of food on a Friday.
The Irishman made him as good a Catholic as himself. This

dog never forsook the sick-bed of his last master, and when he was dead, refused to eat, and died also.'

※§⅋❀

In mid-December 1770 Mr Curry O'Brien bought six heifers from a farmer near Clonmel, County Tipperary to sell in Waterford Market. One heifer's dam had been raised on the Galtee Mountains with a herd of red deer. Unknown to O'Brien, she had inherited her mother's instincts. Driving his cattle through Ballypatrick on the way to market, O'Brien heard the cries of riders and hounds approaching as they hunted a doe nearby. Hearing the pack of hounds, the heifer broke away and made for the nearby mountains. Unknown to the huntsmen, the hounds took up the heifer's trail when the deer and heifers paths crossed tracks. The heifer led them on a chase of 23 miles before being run down. The huntsmen were greatly surprised when they found the hounds challenging a heifer in a bog near Castle Durrow.

※§⅋❀

The *Kerry Journal* of June 1793 reported that a whale had become stranded on shore near the mouth of the Kenmare River and roared so loudly that it could be heard at Killarney Lake four miles away. The echo of its roaring among the hills and mountains terrified people who lived there. The whale was described as being 'seventy feet long and fourteen thick. One of the eyes was more than six horses could draw, and its liver filled two large carts.'

❧❧❧

In his 1756 work *The Ancient and Present State of the County of Kerry*, historian Charles Smith recorded his visit to an orchard on the Godfrey estate at Ballygamboon. He saw many huge apple trees and was particularly taken by one specimen which had a diameter of fifty feet from branch end to branch end. Smith calculated that its canopy area was 1,964 square feet or 218 square yards and, assuming that a standing horse took up a space of around three square yards, estimated that 72 horses could shelter under the drip of the tree.

❧❧❧

Patrick O'Neill of Clonmel, County Tipperary was married – for the seventh time! – at the age of 112 on 15 September 1760. A vegetarian and teetotaller, O'Neill walked to the church without the aid of a stick.

❧❧❧

In the early 1750s historian Charles Smith heard tell of the ingenious way a poor farmer who lived in the mountainside near Castlemaine, County Kerry supplemented his family's diet during hard times. Many eagles nested in the mountains. When the farmer discovered one of the nests, he clipped the eaglets' wings and fixed leather collars round their throats to prevent them swallowing. He checked on them daily and found stores of provisions, such as 'various kinds of excellent fish, wildfowl, rabbits, and hares, which the old ones constantly brought to their young'. He only gave the eaglets enough to keep them alive and took the rest. This allowed the man and his family to survive a hard summer.

※❦❧❦

In April 1747 Mary Saunders from Strancally near Lismore, County Waterford swore an oath before William Smyth of Headborough, County Waterford that she had vomited up a 'four-footed creature, resembling a small water rat, or weasel', after taking some medicine given to her by Cork doctor Dominick Sarsfield. As evidence, she produced the creature before Mr Smyth. It was almost four inches long, one inch wide and black in colour. The author Charles Smith saw the creature himself the following year when it was on display, preserved in a bottle of spirits, in Cork city.

※❦❧❦

Superstitious criminals once believed that the severed hand of an executed criminal had certain properties. On the night of 3 January 1831, thieves attempted to rob Loughcrew House in County Meath. They entered the house armed with a dead man's hand with a lighted candle in it, believing in the superstition that it could not be seen by anyone except those using it and that it would prevent anyone sleeping in the house from waking. The occupants were woken by the noise and the thieves fled, leaving the hand behind them.

❧❧❧

One criminal's novel attempt to evade justice came to light after his scheme failed. Kelly, 'a noted robber', was tried and sentenced to death for his crimes at the Trim Assizes in County Meath in August 1789. While awaiting execution, Kelly cut his blanket into strips four inches wide, joined them together with strong woollen thread and made a double sling around each leg. The ends were fastened at his neck with an iron hook to catch the hangman's noose.

On the day of his execution Kelly walked to the scaffold in the harness he hoped would save him, calmly forgave the hangman for the task he must carry out, and asked him to draw him up close to the pulley and when dead let him down gently. Shortly afterwards the confident criminal's execution was carried out and Kelly pretended to die on the gallows. However, he had not allowed for the stretching of the blanket harness due to his weight and after about eight minutes it sagged and he began to choke for real in the hangman's noose. Kelly struggled and tried to save himself, but to no avail. When he was cut down after death, the harness was discovered, to the astonishment of all, including the hangman, who must have been bribed by Kelly.

❧❧❧

In the eighteenth century a large stream flowed through the kitchen of the mansion owned by Murtagh Oge O'Sullivan of Rossmacowen, Adrigole, County Cork. It entered through a grating in one wall, and discharged itself through a hole in the other. The grating had two purposes: to keep the channel free from rubbish during a flood; and to stop salmon and sea trout going any further when they made their way upstream from Bantry Bay during the spawning season. In this way O'Sullivan was able to catch numerous fish in his kitchen.

Henry Temple, 2nd Viscount Palmerston married the daughter of a Dublin hat maker whom he had met after being thrown from his horse in front of her home. One of Lord Palmerston's limbs was fractured by the fall and he was carried into a nearby house while medical help was sought. The house belonged to Benjamin Mee, a respectable hatter of modest circumstances, and his daughter Mary undertook to nurse the injured man when the doctor said it was too dangerous to move him. They fell in love and were married on 7 January 1783. This couple were the parents of 'England's grand old man' Lord Palmerston, who served as Britain's prime minister for many years.

❧❧❧

A letter in the *Philosophical Transactions of The Royal Society* for 1687 concerns Elizabeth Dooly of Kilkenny. When her mother was pregnant with her, she was knocked to the ground by a cow she was milking and hit on the left temple, 'within an eighth of an inch of her eye', by one of the cow's teats. When the Reverend Dr Ashe, Bishop of Cloyne, saw 13-year-old Elizabeth in January 1687 she 'had a piece of flesh, resembling a cow's teat in size and shape in exactly the same place. It is very red and has a bone in the midst about half its length. It is perforated, and she weeps through it. When she laughs, it winkles up, and contracts to two thirds of its length; and it grows in proportion to the rest of her body. She is as sensible there as in any other part.'

❧❧❧

In August 1800 a yearling calf was heard making an unusual noise close to the River Blackwater near Youghal, County Cork where it had been drinking. On investigation a large pike was found hanging on its nostrils. It had grabbed the calf's nose while it was drinking, and the calf had dragged it about 50 yards from the river and was roaring in pain. On onlooker quickly killed the pike with a large stone and prised it off the calf's nose. When the voracious fish's belly was opened up, a large rat, an entire perch and several other fish were found inside.

❧❦❧

The appearance of an enormous pig at Dublin market was a newsworthy event for newspapers in late February 1845. The pig had been raised in Kildare and was a huge size. It stood five feet tall, measured eleven feet from snout to tail and weighed a little over eleven hundredweight.

❧❦❧

Writing in the seventeenth century, diarist John Dunton describes an unorthodox method of fishing observed in County Westmeath:

I cannot omit acquainting you with one manner of fishing used for diversion in this Lough [near Mullingar]. They take into their boat or cott a goose, and about her body, under her wings, they tie one end of their fishing line, the hook being covered with some bait at the other.

Thus they throw the fishing-goose into the water, who sports and preens herself with seeming pleasure enough, until some unmannerly fish seizes the baited hook and interrupts her diversion by giving her a tug, which douces her almost under water. This commonly frightens her so as to put her to the wing; but if the fish be heavy she is forced to float upon the water, and though in romance the knight generally slays the giant yet, if the pike be of the larger sort, Mrs Goose, without the assistance of the spectators, is sometimes likely to go down to the pike, instead of the pike coming up to her.

❧❧❧

A heifer with a wooden leg would be an unusual sight in any age, so it is no surprise that the appearance of one such animal in Castlebar, County Mayo in late January 1909 amazed all who saw her. The heifer's impediment did not hinder it in any way. The original owner must have had expert surgical skills and had fitted the animal with the wooden leg in a most ingenious way.

When the heifer was about a year and a half old it had an accident which necessitated the amputation of half of one of the front legs, which was successfully carried out. The skin of the injured leg was carefully raised and the injured bone sawn off. When the wound had healed, a padded wooden stump was fitted and the skin drawn down and cemented around it. The operation was a success. When the animal was at ease the wooden leg was not noticeable, but when walking the thud made by the artificial limb at once drew attention. The heifer belonged to a Crossmolina farmer who sold her at a price that any 'four-legged' animal would have reached, making a profit of £2 10s. The heifer was afterwards walked to Westport Quay to be shipped to Glasgow.

Blood periodically gushed from the end of one of Walter Walsh's fingers. It started around Easter 1658 when the 43-year-old innkeeper from Trim, County Meath was racked with pain in his right arm. His hand grew very hot and red and Walsh felt a pricking sensation at the point of his forefinger. When a small speck appeared there, he thought a thorn had lodged in it and made a small cut to remove it.

When he made the incision, blood spurted from it 'in a small, but violent stream'. After it had spent its force it would cease for a while and only drip. Then the wound would gush again, only fading to a drip when its flow ebbed. This alternating sequence continued for twenty-four hours until Walsh passed out from lack of blood and the wound healed itself. When he woke, he found that the pain in his arm had gone.

For the next twelve years the unfortunate innkeeper frequently suffered from these bleeding episodes. He seldom had a respite of more than two months, but the bleeding never occurred more often than every three weeks. Walsh rarely bled less than a 'pottle' (half a gallon) each time. The more often it happened the less he bled, and vice versa. Whenever an attempt was made to staunch the flow of blood it was agony and no remedy was of any use. The bleeding episodes left Walsh very weak. Towards the end of his life he bled very little and the blood looked watery. He died from his affliction on 13 February 1669.

❧❧❧

At about 10 a.m. on 23 April 1900 there was a shower of small fish in the bog close to the coastguard station at Kilcredane, County Clare about three hundred yards from the sea. Several men were working in the bog at the time and reported the unusual occurrence to the officer in charge of the station. He investigated and found about 150 fish had fallen from the sky. They were young sand-eels (*Ammodytes lanceolatus*), which frequent shallow water near the coast at that time of year. The bog was west of the Shannon and the direction of the wind was north-north-west, force 2. It was a fine day, the sky was clear and the wind blew steady.

❧❧❧

Coloured hailstones have sometimes fallen. R.A. Mullan, a solicitor from Newry, was driving a gig near Castlewellan, County Down on 7 May 1885 when he was caught in the middle of a hail shower. Some of the hailstones were red. The colour pervaded the substance of the stones, and on melting, it stained Mullan's fingers.

❧❧❧

An issue of the *Belfast Chronicle* in June 1828 records the fall of a shower of frogs that month. Two gentlemen were sitting talking on a causeway pillar near Bushmills, County Antrim when they were surprised by an unusually sharp shower of rain and frogs falling all around them. The newspaper says that some specimens were preserved in spirits and were exhibited to the curious by the two resident apothecaries in Bushmills.

Saunders' News-Letter of 7 December 1833 contains the report of an unusual romantic event that had occurred in County Limerick a week before. A brother and sister by the name of Conway and a brother and sister by the name of Nash rode into Newcastle West. They rendezvoused at a public house and drank five jugs of good whiskey punch, after which the two men exchanged sisters and they all eloped.

❧❧❧

Read's Weekly Journal of 26 July 1735 says that an 80-year-old Navan woman who had been crippled for years was cured after she went to a local spa. She gained a new lease of life and subsequently married a man two years younger. Since that time, the newspaper reported, large numbers of old women had flocked to the spa.

❧❧❧

James Halfpenny and Daniel McGauran met in a Navan public house on 14 September 1753 and wagered who could drink the most spirits over a three-hour period. It was agreed that the person who got drunk first would foot the bill. Halfpenny drank three quarts and McGauran drank two quarts and a pint, then suddenly collapsed to the floor, seemingly dead. He was carried home and died there before midnight. Halfpenny went to walk home, but met the same fate as his companion and died the next day at ten o'clock.

❧❧❧

On 7 May 1945 a starving Irish prisoner of war staggered into the town of Zwickau in Saxony. As he turned a street corner he collided with an American soldier, whom he accosted with, 'Say, Yank, I'm starving. Have you any food or cigarettes?' The American told the walking skeleton, 'The town is yours, Tommy; take what you want.' He made sure the poor man was fed and looked after.

Exactly a month later the Irishman went into a pub in Newmarket, County Cork. As he neared the counter he noticed the same American soldier he had met in Zwickau. The American too recognised the 'walking skeleton' and dropped his glass on the floor, reeling with shock at the unlikely coincidence of meeting him again. A further surprise was in store for both men when their identities revealed that they were neighbours and boyhood friends. The 'skeleton' was private Denis Herlihy of the Duke of Wellington's Regiment from Boherbue near Newmarket, and the other man was a Sergeant Kelly of the American 3rd Army, whose home was only four miles from Herlihy's. As boys they had gone to the same school but had failed to recognise each other at Zwickau.

❦❦❦

Sarah Dillon from the Coombe in Dublin underwent a Caesarean operation in the Meath Hospital in February 1796. It is said she had been pregnant for two years and two months! A healthy child was removed and the woman made a full recovery.

❦❦❦

Irish immigrant Hannah Reardon was literally a human pin cushion. Her case came to light in 1899, when she was working as a domestic servant to the Nather family of Wilmington, Delaware. After complaining of a sore finger she went to Dr Swithin Chandler for treatment. An examination revealed that there was a needle in her finger which the doctor removed. Four more needles were also found and removed from Hannah's finger. The pain did not lessen and another examination revealed 39 more needles in this one finger. The doctor removed the needles.

Dr Chandler continued operating on Hannah every few days and removed needles from all parts of her body. She was 18 years old, four feet three inches tall, and weighed only 80 pounds. A possible explanation for the presence of so many needles came from Hannah herself. When she was a child in an Irish convent, the small girls stole needles from the larger girls and put them in their mouths to hide them. Some of them were swallowed. Hannah had not worked much before she went to live with the Nathers, and Dr Chandler thought the physical activity might have caused the needles to work to the surface. About twenty of the needles removed from her body were whole and the others were broken in pieces. Her health was quite badly affected, and Hannah was only able to keep liquids down.

❦❧❦

It was once believed that the fairies could substitute a changeling for a natural child. Two Clonmel women, Ellen Cushion and Anastatia Rourke, certainly believed this. They were convinced that a neighbour's child who did not have the use of his limbs was a changeling. On 28 April 1884 they entered the house during the mother's absence and placed the three-year-old child, John Dillon, naked on a hot shovel 'under the impression that this would break the charm'.

The unfortunate child suffered severe burns. The duo were caught and jailed for a few weeks.

❧❦❦❧

Donegal-born Patsy Gallacher enjoyed a successful career as a football player for Celtic. He famously scored one of the strangest goals ever recorded. During the 1925 Scottish Cup Final against Dundee, Gallacher ran into the box with the ball and wedged it between his heels. Then, with the Dundee defenders all around, Gallacher somersaulted over the goal line with the ball and into the net for a goal.

❧❦❦❧

Convicted murderer James Reilly was hanged in Kilmainham Gaol, Dublin on 2 September 1893 – thirty-two years after he had been born there; he had come into the world inside its walls while his mother was serving a sentence for theft. He drew his last breath in the prison where he had first seen the light of day.

❧❦❦❧

When an elephant's tooth was cut up at Read's Cutlers, Dublin, in May 1763 an iron musket ball an inch in diameter was discovered inside. There was no aperture where the ball could have entered.

❧❧❧

In 1935 all the members of a Gaelic football team formed in Porthall, Lifford, County Donegal were called Crawford, and were all related. In one of their games a Crawford was a referee and a Crawford was a linesman.

❧❧❧

About seven o'clock on the morning of 12 July 1793 a Dublin gentleman set out to walk, blindfolded and unaided, from a tavern in Ross Lane to the Rotunda. He made a good start finding his way over Essex Bridge without going astray. The remainder of the journey was more haphazard and the gentleman got lost so often that he had to get down on his hands and knees to feel the flagstones paving the ground to establish his location. His worst blunder was to mistake Henry Street for Britain Street, but he soon discovered his error and retraced his steps. Despite this he reached the Rotunda half an hour after he had set out and laid his hands on the door to win the wager. He then offered to wager twenty guineas that he could find his way back to the tavern blindfolded. No one dared accept his challenge.

❧❧

Donegal-born Michael Malloy (1873–1933) was a homeless alcoholic who is famous for surviving several murder attempts by five acquaintances from a New York speakeasy, who had taken out a large life insurance policy on him. Their attempts to kill Malloy over several weeks were farcical. First, they gave him unlimited credit at the bar, hoping he would literally drink himself to death on the bar's low-grade spirits. When this failed they started to feed him poisonous wood alcohol when he was too drunk to know what he was drinking. This was commonly used as a paint thinner and was not very far removed from anti-freeze. When this had no effect on him either, one of the gang members had the idea of giving Malloy oysters that had been marinated in wood alcohol. This did not kill the Donegal man; neither did a sandwich of rotten sardines mixed with tin shavings, broken glass and carpet tacks.

The gang next decided on a more hands-on approach. One night, when Malloy had passed out drunk, they dumped him in a nearby park when the temperature was some 20°C below freezing. They even threw a bucket of water over him and stripped the clothes from his chest. Certain he would freeze to death, they left the poor man to his fate. They were astounded to find him alive in the bar's basement the next morning. Somehow he had woken and stumbled back to the warmth of the speakeasy.

On the sixth attempt they ran him over with a car after he had passed out from drinking. They were sure he was dead, but could not collect the insurance when they could not find his body. As a desperate measure they found another drunk who resembled Malloy and ran him over too, but had to flee the scene when someone spotted them. The substitute survived with no memory of what had happened to him or any realisation of how lucky he was. Malloy surprised them again by turning up at the bar a few days later with a few broken bones and no recollection of anything either. A good Samaritan had found him and brought him to a hospital, where he had been recovering.

The gang finally managed to kill Malloy on 22 February 1933. When he had again passed out from drinking, they stuck a pipe in his mouth and connected it to a gas jet. Malloy was dead in minutes. Rumours of the gang's epic undertaking spread through the New York underworld and soon reached the police. They investigated the unlikely story and soon rounded up the gang. Most of them were executed.

❦❦❦

In 1839 quintuplets were born to Mrs Patrick O'Phelan of Dunkerrin, County Offaly. Four sons and a daughter were safely delivered. They all survived. Sixteen months before, Mrs Phelan had had triplets – two daughters and a son. In other words, she bore eight children in a year and a half.

❦❦❦

Bagnel Bentley, a 97-year-old tailor from Dunshaughlin, County Meath married 99-year-old Catherine Sheppard from Skreen in November 1764. The bride had had three husbands before Bentley, the last of whom had died in July 1764 aged 104.

❦❦❦

At the beginning of 1794 a humorous incident occurred in the grounds of Dublin Castle. Some time before, a farmer had bought an old retired troop horse. As it was a quiet animal, the farmer let his daughter ride it and sent her to the city with milk. One day she arrived at the Exchange at the time the guard was changing at nearby Dublin Castle. The horse, hearing familiar music, became uncontrollable and bolted into the Castle Yard, 'snuffing and snorting', with his rider and her milk pails, and took its place in the midst of the ranks, to the great amusement of all present.

❦❦❦

Two dogs, a spaniel and a pointer, belonging to a Mr Bishop of County Waterford in August 1797 chased a hare into a local wood. They continued to chase it into the night. In the dark, they fell into a pit and could not get out. They were found alive 17 days later and made a full recovery.

❧❦❧

A man in Marrowbone Lane in Dublin had an argument with his wife in July 1763 and beat her savagely with a cabbage stalk. Enraged by her treatment, the woman assembled some of her female friends and they attacked and beat the man with cabbage stalks in revenge. The husband was so severely injured that he died the next day.

❧❦❧

A bizarre accident took place in the Phoenix Park, Dublin in March 1796. Two men riding spirited horses at full gallop from opposite directions collided. The horses met head-on and died instantly, while the riders were thrown some distance, and one of them was badly injured.

❧❦❧

In August 1792 a curious wager was decided in Dublin. Dingle, a 'purblind brush-maker' and a noted glutton, undertook to compete against a bulldog in eating tripe. Twelve pounds of tripe was to be divided between man and dog, and the winner would be the one who finished first. Dingle's opponents tried to rig the contest, putting all the fat into his tripe, along with strips cut from a pair of old leather breeches to ruin his appetite.

Dingle won easily despite the tampering, eating eight pounds of tripe in fifteen minutes, while the dog took twenty minutes to eat the other four pounds. Afterwards he undertook to drink (for another wager) twelve quarts of ale in six draughts inside four hours. He performed the feat in three hours – despite the addition of an unfortunate small live mouse, which a mischievous onlooker put into his last flagon.

❧❦❧

The following curious description was painted on a board a few miles from Dublin in 1786: 'Good grass for horses on the following terms: – Long-tails at 3s.6d. and Short-tails at half a crown a week.' The explanation given for the difference in price was that long-tailed horses could, by whisking flies away, always feed undisturbed, but short-tailed horses could not do that and were so tormented in the daytime that they could not feed.

❧❦❧

Alfred Tennyson's poem 'To-morrow' was inspired by a story told him by Aubrey de Vere. The well-preserved body of a young man was found in a Connemara bog in the nineteenth century. His identity was a mystery until an old woman came along and recognised it as that of her young lover, who had disappeared sixty years before.

❧❧❧

On 9 July 1795 a terrible tragedy took place near Moyvane, County Kerry. Two men were swimming in the Galey River when one suddenly disappeared. His friend raised the alarm, and after a careful search the body was found. A large eel was coiled around the corpse's neck, biting at its throat. The only way to separate the eel from the body was to cut off its head. It measured five and a half feet long and weighed 36 pounds.

❧❧❧

Around 1795 a Hessian (German) regiment was stationed in Longford town at the Lower Barracks. It is said that the men were 'extremely sensitive to the least rebuke' and suicides were a daily occurrence among them. One morning alone no fewer than fifteen soldiers were found to have taken their own lives. With such a high number of suicides the regiment was disbanded and sent back to Germany.

❧❧❧

Preserved in the little village of Timahoe in County Laois is one of the finest round towers in Ireland. In 1837, for a dare, a young man climbed the tower without any help. When he reached the top of the conical roof he celebrated by standing on his head.

❧❧❧

A cocker bitch belonging to James Stackpoole Malone of Castle Malone in County Clare suckled two young hares in 1790. The dog was as careful with the leverets as if they were her own puppies.

❧❧❧

A wild duck built her nest forty feet high in a fir tree near Loughlinstown in County Meath in 1744. In May of that year she managed to bring her young ducklings down safely to a nearby pond.

❧❧❧

Workmen employed by Reverend Dickson at Monroe Glebe near Dungarvan, County Waterford in 1818 to sink a well in the limestone made a curious discovery. At a depth of thirty-six feet they found large numbers of living frogs. The rock appeared to be a solid mass without any passage through which the animals could have entered.

❧❧❧

It is said that Castle Archdale, County Fermanagh was built in 1773 from stone taken from nearby monastic ruins. As a result it was widely believed that no heir would ever be born within its walls – a prediction that has been proved accurate so far.

❧❧❧❧

At Crosslane, near Enniskillen, County Fermanagh, a peculiar ash tree became an object of curiosity in 1762. It carried two growths of leaves each year. The tree shed the first growth in July. Then the second sprouted and fell again in the autumn, like any other tree. The ash had done this for the previous twenty years.

❧❧❧❧

A huge lobster was caught near Lambay Island, County Dublin in June 1795. The formidable beast weighed fifteen pounds and was described as being 'nearly as large as a small lamb'. Its shell was covered with barnacles, and the feelers were nearly a yard long. It was sold on the spot to a gentleman for two guineas.

❧❧❧❧

Troop Sergeant Major Matthew Marshall of the 6th Dragoons (better known as the Inniskillings) from County Down survived terrible injuries he received at the Battle of Waterloo on 18 June 1815. The Inniskillings made several brilliant charges against the French, and during one counter-attack they were cut off by the enemy. In the desperate fighting a sword blow broke Marshall's left arm.

As he rode on, an enemy lance pierced his right side and knocked him off his horse. As he fell, he received another heavy blow to the body, and another broke his right thigh. He hit the ground and briefly fell unconscious, only coming to when the hooves of the enemy's horses trod on his mangled body as they passed over him. When the way became clearer Marshall saw a horse without a rider and crawled towards it in agony.

He was about to mount it when a French trooper galloped up and cut him down, inflicting several severe wounds on him. This part of the battlefield being again in French control, an enemy artillery man used Marshall's body as a resting place for his foot while he reloaded his gun. Marshall lay on the battlefield for two days and three nights, but he survived his nineteen wounds. On his return home to Ireland, he was discharged with a generous pension of two shillings a day and settled in Belfast, where he died in 1825 at the age of fifty.

❧❧❧

In 1793 Daniel Ruckle of Ballingrane, County Limerick had a hen that laid three eggs a day. Each egg had two yolks and two whites separate from each other. Twelve of these eggs were put under another hen. When the eggs hatched, twenty-four cock chicks emerged.

❧❧❧

A peculiar penknife with 384 blades was made under very unusual circumstances by John Hayes, who worked for Colgan's cutlers in Limerick. In 1830 Hayes made a dagger to gift to a friend. Arriving at the house where the presentation was going to take place, Hayes found his friend involved in a row and went to his aid. He used the dagger on one of the assailants, killing him instantly. He was arrested and convicted of the crime. Through his employer's influence he escaped the most extreme sentence of the law and was instead condemned to a term of imprisonment on board a convict ship hulk at Cobh. It was during this confinement in the vessel that Hayes made this penknife, which he intended to be presented to the Lord Lieutenant and was afterwards exhibited in Paris, London, Dublin and Edinburgh.

❧❧❧

While two gentlemen were crossing the magnificent railway viaduct over the River Boyne at Drogheda, County Louth in March 1858, along with an eighteen-month-old water spaniel, his owner praised its intrepid nature and fearlessness. His friend jokingly asked if he thought the dog would follow his walking stick if he threw it from where they stood. The owner responded by a grave shake of the head and his friend threw the stick from the bridge. Without hesitation the spaniel dashed after it through the bars and disappeared, falling into the water 102 feet below. Its owner was shocked and believed that the poor animal was dead. Shortly afterwards the dog was spotted on the river bank carrying the walking stick, patiently waiting the arrival of its master. The lucky dog had not suffered the slightest injury from its extraordinary leap.

❦❦❦

There are many examples of women hiding their gender to serve as soldiers or sailors. Irish-born Hannah Witney served over five years as a marine on board different ships disguised as a man. She only revealed her gender in October 1761 after being picked up in Plymouth by a press-gang and committed to the town's prison. She was so disgusted by being jailed she disclosed her secret and was freed, but not before telling the astonished official that she would not have made her sex known if she had not been grabbed by the press-gang.

❦❦❦

A soldier had a narrow escape at Enniskillen, County Fermanagh in July 1846. He was thirty feet below ground repairing a stone well in the county jail beneath some timber beams stretched across the well when the upper part of the walling gave way. Fortunately the stones fell on the sturdy beams and formed an arch and the soldier below was unhurt. It was feared the whole arch would give way if the stones were removed. An army engineer and a detachment of troops were called in to rescue the unfortunate man.

The engineer advised that a tunnel be dug some way from the well towards the spot where the trapped man was and the work quickly got under way. Meanwhile the trapped man's fellow worker persisted in attempting to free him by carefully removing stones, which he sent up in a bucket. Eventually he made a hole large enough for his friend to be pulled through and the trapped man was freed eight hours after being buried alive.

❦❦❦

The daring ingenuity of an Irish thief who fell foul of the Greenock police made news in January 1880. When caught the man feigned a comatose state. His ruse did not fool the Greenock police surgeon and a state of consciousness was quickly induced. The thief was transported to the town where, it was alleged, he had committed a robbery, and jailed there to await trial. He soon escaped the jail and fled. A few days later he was caught red-handed and taken into custody, but not before some hard blows had been exchanged between him and the constables. Bleeding from the mouth as a result of a whack from a baton, the Irishman was brought before a police surgeon who did not know his tricks.

The cunning thief pretended to be dying, and his acting was so convincing that the surgeon really believed the thief had died in front of him. After laying out the 'dead' man in the mortuary, minus his boots, the surgeon hurried off to report the fatal assault by the police. The mortuary was attached to the police station and the surgeon left the door ajar. After the surgeon made his report to the ranking officer the policemen involved in the assault were detained. When this officer and the surgeon returned to the mortuary to examine the corpse it was gone! The Irishman had made another escape.

❧❧❧

Patrick Woods and his wife and six children lived in a house in Chapel Lane in Armagh town. On 3 January 1829 they narrowly escaped death when the house's roof collapsed. That they escaped at all was due to a terrifying dream Patrick Woods had had. For a few nights before the collapse he had slept very badly and on the night it happened he had had such bad dreams he got up at five o'clock, dressed himself, got his wife and children up and forced them out of the house. Once his family was safely outside, Woods looked back and saw that he had forgotten to close the house door. He went back to shut it. As soon as his hand touched the latch he heard the timbers give way and the entire roof fell in with a 'frightful crash'. In daylight the complete destruction of the house was clear to see. If the family had been inside when the roof collapsed they would have all been killed. Ironically, the house had undergone major repairs only a short time before.

❧❧❧

In October 1858 a man named Power from Castlecomer, County Kilkenny went out to fly a very large kite. In the high wind it quickly ascended until the full length of cord had run out. By some freak accident the cord became entangled around Power's hand and he was helplessly dragged nearly half a mile by the kite. The cord had cut right to the bone. The local Anglican clergyman, Reverend Penrose, saw Power running along and shouting for help.

Penrose could not believe his eyes when he saw Power actually lifted off the ground by the kite. He gave chase but could not close the distance fast enough to help the unfortunate man. 'Let go!' he shouted, 'There was a man killed in a thunderstorm by the lightning of a kite!' When Power heard this he redoubled his shouts for help and made another desperate attempt to free himself. All his efforts were useless. The kite pulled Power head first into a high stone wall, which was a blessing in disguise. The wall was topped by sharp flat stones, which cut the cord and set free both kite and man. The unfortunate Power was said to have been almost lifeless with 'fatigue and fright'.

❧❧

The *Freeman's Journal* of 1 September 1795 carries wonderful proof of the saying that no good deed goes unpunished. Late one night a drunken woman was making her way home towards O'Connell Bridge, Dublin when she stopped to listen to a blind female musician playing a fiddle to earn money from passers-by. The woman took pity on the musician and rummaged in her pockets for a few small coins to give her, accidentally dropping some money. The woman stooped down and searched for it by the light of the fiddler woman's lantern.

Unfortunately, and unbeknownst to her, a blazing lantern set fire to her headwear. She would have been seriously burnt if a gentleman passing by had not spotted her on fire and quickly pushed her into a puddle, rolling her over until the fire was out. No sooner than the fire was out the woman recovered from her soaking and started cursing and hitting him. She would have set the police or night watch on him if he had not prudently made a quick exit.

❧❧❧

While visiting a friend on the north coast on 25 May 1814, the weather being fine, a Belfast gentleman hired a boat and two men to row it. He decided to visit a small island nearby that was covered at high water during spring tides. There he hoped to pick up seashells and other curiosities. After dropping him off, the boatmen sought permission to visit another nearby island and promised to get him some oysters there. Believing they would not be away long, he gave them permission to go.

Left on his own the gentleman began his hunt for curiosities and lost all track of time. Suddenly, to his horror, he noticed that the tide was coming in and had already risen two feet above the shoreline. In a short time, he realised, it would completely cover the island. With the boat and boatmen nowhere to be seen the gentleman was naturally very alarmed at the situation. Worse still, he could not swim and it was over half a mile to shore.

At this point he spotted several large stones that lay scattered about the island, and a plan began to form. His only chance, slim though it was, might be to stack up the stones as high as he dared and use this shaky platform to stand on. Some of the stones were too heavy to lift, but he managed to roll six of the largest together to form a foundation for his tower. Using this as a base, he built up rows of the heaviest stones he could lift. In this way he built a tower six feet high and capped it with a large flat stone.

With great difficulty and nervousness he clambered up the precarious structure to reach its high point. Standing on the summit, he tied a white handkerchief to the end of his cane and waved it as a distress signal in the hope that someone would see it. Then he waited for the tide to submerge the island and test his tower's strength. The cane and handkerchief saved his life. The two boatmen were at the other side of another island when they saw the waving handkerchief and immediately put out to sea to investigate.

To their astonishment the signal came from the gentleman 'whose perilous situation they had so strangely forgotten'. By the time the pair spotted the handkerchief the tide had just reached the base of the tower and although they rowed hard to get back to the island it had risen a considerable way up the tower. Had another half an hour elapsed before their return it was likely the gentleman would have drowned. The boatmen apologised profusely for their negligence and the gentleman, finding himself safe at last, was happy to let the matter drop. Riding near the place two years later the gentleman was amazed to see that his rough stone tower was still standing.

❧❦❧

Six vicious murderers were captured because of the homing instincts of a dog they left behind at a crime scene. A long paragraph in the *Freeman's Journal* of 17 April 1794 details their crime and capture. In an unnamed part of Leinster the bandits attacked a household in the absence of the farmer, who had gone to a fair. His wife and child and two servants were left in the house. The thieves attacked and killed the two servants first. The farmer's wife and child happened to be upstairs when the thieves attacked. When the woman heard them killing her servants she acted quickly, hiding her child in a bed and piling clothes on it. Then she forced herself up a chimney and hid.

After killing the servants, the bandits searched every part of the house for the woman, but did not find her. However, they discovered the child and tortured it to death in the hopes of drawing the woman out from her hiding place. The poor woman forced herself to resist the heartbreaking screams of her child, as she knew she would not have been able to save the child, and what was the use of a pointless death? After stripping the house of its valuables the murderers fled, but accidentally left behind a dog that belonged to one of them.

The scene that lay in wait for the farmer is unimaginable. On his return he could not get into the house and knew something was wrong. He raised the alarm and some neighbours helped him break into the house, where he discovered the dead bodies of his servants and child. Hearing his voice, his wife came down from the chimney. The murderers' dog was secured and a magistrate sent for. After some discussion they decided the best way of tracking down the men was to let the dog find its own way home. As an added incentive they cut off the poor animal's ears and part of its tail and set it loose.

They tracked the howling dog all the way to a house a long distance away, and heard the woman of the house uttering curses against those who had cruelly maltreated her dog. The trackers signalled the rest of the farmer's neighbours to advance. They surrounded the house, captured all the men inside, who were caught unawares while dividing the booty they had taken, and dragged them off to jail.

Scaffolding was erected around the spire of St Patrick's Cathedral, Dublin in 1808 to repair storm damage. On

20 June, for the small wager of a gallon of porter, a local man named Moore, a roofer by trade, bet he could climb to the ball on the damaged spire. Moore climbed the scaffolding, which stopped within twelve feet of his destination. Using his hands and knees, Moore clambered up and sat astride the section that had 'been bent into a horizontal position' by the storm.

He had hardly done so when the structure gave way, and man and all fell through the scaffolding. The daring man was lucky. His clothes caught in the damaged timbers of one of the scaffolding stages, leaving him hanging 'between heaven and earth'. The section of spire and stone ball fell from a height of two hundred feet and buried itself nearly a yard into the ground at the foot of the cathedral. Moore soon freed himself and climbed down triumphantly and was carried to the nearest public house to celebrate his extraordinary exploit.

❧❧❧

One of the most celebrated jewellery shops to cater to the affluent in Dublin was Law's on O'Connell Street at the corner of Eden Quay. On each side of the entrance was a single sheet of glass, behind which were magnificent displays of costly silverware, gems and watches. In May 1847 an unassuming elderly gentleman stood at one of the windows admiring the valuables. He had an umbrella, which he carried beneath his arm in a horizontal position. Unfortunately the iron tip of the umbrella was far too near the expensive sheet of glass. A young man came running down the footpath, violently jostling the elderly man, and the pane was smashed by the point of the umbrella. The young man fled down Eden Quay and disappeared, leaving the elderly gentleman to deal with the fall-out.

Mr Law and his assistants cornered the gentleman and blamed him for the damage. In his defence he blamed the ruffian who had pushed him, but Law demanded the gentleman pay £9 to replace the broken window, and threatened to call the police. The gentleman held his ground, bluntly stating that he was not at fault and refusing to pay. Law refused to let him leave until his window was paid for. The gentleman introduced himself as James Ridley from Lincoln's Inn Fields in London, explained that he had just arrived from England to purchase extensive estates in the west of Ireland, and threatened to sue for ample damages if he was not allowed to depart.

Seeing that Law was about to send for the police, Ridley produced a £100 Bank of England note and told the 'obdurate scoundrel' to take the cost of his window out of that 'at his peril'. Law disregarded the threat, deducted £9, and gave £91 back to Ridley, who left vowing vengeance. The threatened legal proceedings never followed and subsequent enquiries seeking to find Ridley in London drew a blank. The reason? The £100 bank note was a forgery and Law had been the unwitting dupe of a clever scam.

❧❧

Police magistrate Frank Thorpe Porter had been away from his home on holiday at a friend's house in Donabate, north Dublin, for a week in the 1850s. On the morning of his return to work he went straight from Donabate to court in Dublin to hear cases instead of going home. One case involved a youth arrested at four o'clock that morning on Rathmines Road, carrying a large amount of clothes, and charged with having stolen or unlawfully obtaining them.

When Porter called on the youth to account how he came by the clothes, he refused, merely saying 'that Porter would know soon enough'. Porter ordered him jailed for a week, then sent to Glencree Juvenile Reformatory for three years. Returning home to his house in Rathmines that evening, Porter learned a large amount of clothing had been stolen from a washing line in the back yard the night before.

❦❧❦

In February 1773, 14-year-old Anne Mulligan of Roxberry went to visit a neighbour's house one evening and returned home that night having completely lost her voice. She remained that way until May 1777, when friends brought her to Dr Connell of Bunnoe, Cavan. Dr Connell was known as the 'mad doctor' on account of his unusual methods, and his treatment of Anne showed how unorthodox he was. The doctor heard her story and examined the girl, then brought her into his dining room and locked the door. He sat her at one end of the table, then sat opposite. He began by distorting his features in 'a shocking manner' intended to frighten the girl. After some time he jumped up, grabbed a dagger that was hanging over the mantelpiece, and ran at Anne, swearing that he was going to kill her. She dropped to her knees, begging him to spare her life, then fainted. On coming to she completely regained her speech and never lost it again.

❦❦❦

The position of Recorder of Dublin was a judicial office in pre-independence Ireland. The office holder was in effect chief magistrate for Dublin, with responsibility for hearing civil and legal cases and for keeping the peace. William Walker held this post from 1794 until his death in 1820. He was a singular character and dealt justice in his own unique way. One day a groom employed by a neighbour of Walker's was tried before him for stealing a large bag of oats from his master's stable, which was in a lane at the back of Dominick Street.

Having been caught red-handed, the accused was naturally convicted. Walker sentenced the man to imprisonment for three months and added that the groom was to be publicly whipped from one end of the lane to the other end and back again at the start and finish of his prison sentence, as Walker was 'determined with the help of providence, to put a stop to oat-stealing in that lane'. His strong feelings about this were no doubt due to the fact that his own stable was in the same lane.

The Recorder was a great amateur farmer and had a country house and small farm near Harold's Cross. He took pride in his abundant crop of early hay. On one occasion when he attended the assizes, he was extremely annoyed to find that there were twenty cases of larceny waiting to be tried just when he was in a hurry to tend to three acres of cut meadow. As he feared that the haymaking would either be neglected or mismanaged in his absence, Walker decided on a stratagem to clear his workload.

Learning that an old offender was on his list he sent the man a hint through the clerk of the court advising him that he would get a short sentence if he pleaded guilty. When the old criminal came before Walker he pleaded guilty and was sentenced to only three months in jail. When the other prisoners learned how leniently he had been treated they all pleaded guilty in turn. Walker deferred sentencing the men until each had been dealt with. Then all the guilty men were placed in the dock and – to their horror – sentenced to seven years' transportation to Australia. Walker was delighted and was able to return quickly to his farming activities.

❧❧❧

Present-day Christchurch Place in the shadow of Dublin's great cathedral was once known as Skinner's Row, and many goldsmiths and jewellers were located on the street. One of the most prominent was Matthew West. He gave considerable employment to a skilful gem-setter named Delandre, who lived in the upper part of a house in Great Ship Street. In 1811 a wealthy client brought a diamond worth £950 to West and asked him to set it in a particular style.

Delandre was entrusted with the diamond and instructed how to proceed. He took it to his workroom at home, which overlooked a burial ground from which it was divided by a wall topped with broken glass. The weather being very warm, Delandre opened the window closest to his bench and went back to work. He put pressure on the diamond while setting it into position and the stone flew out of the window. Keeping an eye on the ground outside, Delandre alerted his family and a search was organised for the gem. Every inch of the area was searched.

A large area was swept and the sweepings were sifted. The top of the wall was also carefully brushed, but the diamond could not be found. With a heavy heart Delandre informed West of the disastrous loss of the valuable gem. The jeweller took its loss calmly and accepted Delandre's story. West undertook to continue to give employment to the gem-setter and his son, but to make regular deductions to pay for an insurance policy on Delandre's life and to recover the value of the gem. Delandre willingly agreed to his terms. Over a number of years the value of the diamond was repaid and West handed over the insurance policy to Delandre to benefit his family when the old man died.

The story of the Ship Street diamond had a curious ending in 1842. Repairs were being made at the back of Delandre's home. Among the jobs carried out was replastering the boundary wall and replacing the glass on the top of the wall. One of the workmen removed the old broken glass from the wall and found the famous missing diamond lodged in the neck of a pint bottle that had been set in plaster, mouth downwards. It had formed a trap in which the diamond had been caught after falling from the window.

By this time Matthew West was dead, but Delandre was still alive. He paid the finder a reward and both men made a sworn statement before a magistrate concerning its discovery. His debt to West being long since paid, the elderly man was now entitled to the diamond and richer by the contents of this unique 31-year-old savings bank.

❧❧❧

The true tale of a missing £1,000 note is a delightful part of the history of the Bank of Ireland. In the 1830s a Dublin woman named Mrs Pearce had a £1,000 note which she kept hidden in a wardrobe in her bedroom. When the note disappeared without trace Mrs Pearce suspected a servant girl of the theft and dismissed her. The story would have ended there if it had not come to the attention of the bank's governor, William Chaigneau Colvill.

He heard of Mrs Pearce's loss and made his own investigation. Mr Colvill visited Mrs Pearce's house and examined the wardrobe. He removed a few loose boards and found the nest of a mouse in the base of the wardrobe. It was lined with white paper material, which the Governor recognised as the paper the bank used. The nest was carefully removed and inspected by the bank's printers. Extraordinarily, they found the number of the missing bank note. A new note was issued to Mrs Pearce on the understanding that the girl who had been wrongly accused of theft be either reinstated or compensated. After the death of Mrs Pearce years later, her executors presented a gold watch and a brooch to Governor Colvill.

The Skinner's Row jeweller Matthew West lived in Harcourt Street, Dublin and was known to leave large sums of money in his wife's care. One morning in 1817 a stylish liveried servant entered the jewellery premises and asked if his master, Captain Marmaduke Wilson, had been there. He explained that his master intended to purchase some plate and had arranged to meet him at West's. The servant described Captain Wilson as a fine-looking man, who had lost his right arm at the Battle of Waterloo. The man added that he had to deliver a message elsewhere but would be back in ten minutes and requested West to explain his absence if the captain arrived in the meantime.

Some time later the heralded Captain Wilson arrived. He was indeed a dashing military man. He wore a frogged coat with a Waterloo ribbon pinned to it, and had a fine moustache. The former soldier explained that he was moving to a property in County Monaghan and wanted to set up residence in style, but with economy. He had heard that West had a large stock of second-hand silverware and wished to buy some from which the crestings could be obliterated and his own crest substituted. As an example Captain Wilson flourished a silver snuff box on which a crest was engraved with his initials beneath it.

When his servant returned, both men were shown a large selection of silverware. Wilson picked out a good amount and bargained the price down to £140. He asked West to pack up the silverware in his servant's basket so that he could show his wife the silverware before the crests were altered. He also asked West to be his secretary and to write to Mrs Wilson for the payment. He would send his servant for the money, and when he bought it back, West would let him take the basket. The jeweller put pen to paper and wrote the following note at Captain Wilson's dictation: 'Dear Maria, I have bought some second-hand plate, of which, I think, you will approve. Send me, by bearer, £140.'

Wilson added, 'Just put my initials, M.W. Is it not very curious, that our initials are the same?' Then he took the pen in his left hand and made a rough circle in the left-hand corner, which he said was his private mark. Captain Wilson told his servant to fetch the money and make haste while he remained there. He waited for some time and seemed very impatient at his servant's delay. Finally Captain Wilson could wait no longer and said his goodbyes to West, asking him to let the servant have the basket when he returned with the money. The servant did not come for the plate, and it remained packed and ready for delivery on the arrival of the purchase money. Late in the afternoon West went home, and after dining, was asked by his wife 'What second-hand plate was it that you bought today?'

'I bought none,' he replied, 'but I sold some, and it was to have been taken away at once, but I suppose it will be sent for tomorrow.'

'And why,' asked his wife, 'did you send to me for one hundred and forty pounds? Here is your note, which a servant in livery brought, and I gave him the money.' Matthew West groaned and realised he had been tricked by clever swindlers. No trace of the 'Waterloo' captain or his servant was ever found. In all probability the 'Captain Wilson' likely only pretended to have one arm, and used both his hands to take off his false moustache and change his appearance minutes after leaving West.

❦

At Anner Mill near Clonmel, County Tipperary, a gardener found a strange-looking object hanging from a branch of an apple tree in December 1901. It was nearly round, about as large as a football and streaked all over with the brightest colours. He soon discovered that it was a wasps' nest, but he was puzzled by its odd colouring. The explanation was simple. The gardener's employer had bought a large amount of long paper shavings of different colours – red, blue, green, yellow and white – which he hung over his strawberry beds to protect the fruit from the attentions of insects and birds.

Instead of being warned off by the coloured streamers, a colony of wasps had reduced the paper to pulp and carried it away to use to build their nest, which quickly grew under the united efforts of an army of little artists.

❧❧❧

For some years prior to 1842 the number of persons found drowned in the county of Dublin was far greater than might be expected. The cases of drowning in the Royal Canal to the north of the city and the Grand Canal to the south were far more numerous than could be attributed to violence, drunkenness, suicide or accident. It also seemed that the Grand Canal was by far the more destructive to life and the bank that lay in the county (rather than the city) jurisdiction possessed some attraction for the corpses, as they were almost always taken out on the county side.

On the morning of 11 March 1842 a young man named Kinsella was heading to work from his home at Dolphin's Barn when he was stopped at the canal bridge by a constable and ordered to be a juror at an inquest that was about to be held nearby. It was concerning the body of an old man that had just been taken from the canal. Kinsella tried to escape the duty, but was told it would be very short as there were no marks of violence on the corpse and would merely be a case of 'found drowned'.

The coroner swore in the jury and conducted them to the room where they were required by law to view the body. As soon as Kinsella saw the corpse he rushed forward, dropped to his knees beside it, and exclaimed: 'My father! We buried

him on this day week in the Hospital Fields. He had no
business in the canal, and them old clothes never belonged
to him!'

The doctor and coroner vainly tried to convince Kinsella
that he was mistaken, but he remained adamant. An
investigation followed and it emerged that the coroner and
doctor were paid by the number of inquests held. They had
bumped up the numbers by disinterring recently buried
bodies, dressing them up in old clothes and throwing them
in the canal. The bodies were always quickly discovered
and taken out on the county side to swell their coffers. The
coroner and doctor were convicted of conspiring to defraud.

❦

The Royal Navy sloop *Swallow* fought a heroic action
against two more heavily armed French ships from Fréjus
on 16 June 1812. On board were 26-year-old Waterford sailor
Joseph Phelan and his wife. She was stationed below deck, as
was usual when women aboard in the time of battle helped
the surgeon take care of the wounded. While Mrs Phelan was
looking after a fatally wounded mess mate of her husband's
she learned that Joseph had been wounded on deck.

She raced topside to be with him and held him in her
arms as he lay dying. Phelan weakly raised his head to kiss
her and she burst into a flood of tears, and told her husband
to take courage, as 'all would yet be well'. The poor woman
had hardly pronounced the last syllable when a cannonball
took off her head. The poor sailor, who was closely wrapped
in her arms, opened his eyes once more, then shut them for

ever. His wife had only recently given birth to a fine son, Thomas, and now he was an orphan.

When the action ceased the sailors were particularly affected by the child's fate. 'They all agreed he should have a hundred fathers,' but feared he would die without a wet nurse or mother to feed him. Fortunately there was on board a Maltese goat belonging to the officers, which had plenty of milk. The child was allowed to suckle her. It worked and the child thrived. The goat was a placid creature and became so comfortable with the child suckling her that she even lay down when the baby was brought to her. Thomas's unfortunate parents were sewn into one hammock and buried at sea.

❦❦❦

Mary Tudor and Christian Wilson were both the children of successful goldsmiths on Skinner's Row. They fell in love, but Mary's father, Dick, tried to split them up the moment he learned of their romance. He sent her to stay with relatives in Kilmore, County Wexford. After several weeks Christian discovered where Mary was staying and secretly planned a trip to see her. He had learned that the small fast boats that traded between Wexford and Dublin could make the run in a few hours if aided by a fair wind. He told his father he wished to visit a friend in Drogheda and got permission to go there for a few days. Instead he took passage on a trading boat to Wexford and visited Mary.

On the same night Christian sailed, Dick Tudor's shop was robbed. Two of the thieves were caught and it was discovered that they had been seen in Christian's company in a public house that night. Suspicion fell on the missing youth about his involvement in the robbery. It did not help when it came to light that he had not gone to Drogheda. When Christian returned a few days later his father was furious – as was Mary's when he learned where Christian had been. After badly beating a jealous rival for Mary's affection who had taunted him with involvement in the theft, Christian had to flee rather than face prison.

His father arranged passage to the West Indies and Christian had just enough time to write a letter to Mary before he left. She doggedly sought the truth surrounding the robbery and proved that Christian was entirely innocent of any involvement. Witnesses on the trading ship Christian had taken to Wexford confirmed that they had left hours before the robbery. Additionally, the captured thieves swore he had not been part of the gang. They had sought out his company to try to gain intelligence about Tudor's premises. The Tudor and Wilson families were reconciled. More good news followed. The man Christian beat up recovered and would not make any charges against Christian.

It was many months before it was discovered that Christian's ship never reached its intended destination and all aboard were believed lost at sea. Mary alone refused to believe that Christian was dead and refused the unwanted advances of other suitors. Eight years later a mutual friend of the two families persuaded them to accompany him to Cork Hill. There they watched newly arrived troops marching in to relieve the guard at Dublin Castle, and were delighted to see Christian, now Captain Wilson of the 60th Regiment, leading his own company. He and other survivors from his ship had been rescued from a small boat by a British frigate carrying Lord Carlisle to America. The nobleman took an interest in the unassuming youth, who made himself useful aboard the ship. On arrival in America he secured Christian a commission in the army. Now reunited after so many years, the couple's love had not faded and they were married.

❧❧

John Harvey Boteler was a midshipman aboard the frigate *Orantes*. While the ship was at Cork during the harsh winter of 1813/14, Boteler was ordered ashore to accompany a press-gang. They had intelligence that that a lot of seamen were hiding at a certain small public house in Cobh and made their way to the spot. Boteler recorded that the press-gang secured a number of 'very prime hands' after a short fight. A wake was going on in the public house and a number of women were howling over a coffin, where a corpse was laid out. The lieutenant leading the *Orantes* press-gang did not believe them, 'and sure enough out popped a seaman'. The 'corpse' was quickly press-ganged with his friends.

❧❧

A purse was found inside a large codfish in Cobh police barracks, County Cork on 23 November 1911 as it was being prepared for cooking. The strange discovery was made by a cook as he cleaned the fish. The leather purse contained several silver coins dating from Queen Victoria's reign. It also contained a small document, which could not be read, because the paper had gone to pulp inside the fish's belly. The purse itself was in a good state of preservation. The codfish had been caught by a fishing boat from Arklow off the southern coast.

An extraordinary three-way duel took place near Waterford in May 1797. A young doctor from the city, believing his honour had been insulted by two officers, demanded satisfaction. In order to make short work of it, he proposed to fight them both at once with pistols. His challenge was accepted and all three of them met the next morning. The doctor stood between his adversaries, with a pistol in each hand pointed at both. All the combatants fell at the first shots. The doctor was wounded in the upper chest. One of his opponents was shot through the knee, and the other in his right side. All three men recovered.

❦❦❦

How Skellig Mohr, a goat from the rugged mountains of County Kerry, ended up as the mascot of the American battleship *Vermont* is a curious tale. The goat was imported in 1906 for ceremonial purposes by 'Colonel' Roger F. Scannell, then president of the Boston-based Knights of St Brendan. When in-fighting and dissent split the organisation the following year, Scannell founded another society and took the goat with him. The two societies fought a bitter battle in the courts over the rightful ownership of the Kerry goat until wiser heads prevailed and the factions compromised and made a present of the animal to the *Vermont*. Skellig Mohr was welcomed to its new home in a special ceremony on the warship's quarterdeck on 16 March 1909.

❦❦❦

The coal shortage in Ireland in February 1947 became so desperate that the furnaces providing heat to the reptile house in Dublin Zoo were shut down on 13 February. The snakes started to freeze, according to newspaper reports, which described how the keeper carried two boas around under his overcoat to keep them from freezing. The man said the other snakes were as stiff as Bologna sausage and were being put in warm water from 'time to time' to thaw them out.

❧❧❧

A young Irishman emigrated to America in 1909 but decided to return home three months later after he saw a snake in a field where he was working. Terence Breen was working on the farm of Nicholas Sproull in Taylortown, New Jersey when he saw his first snake while cutting fodder with a scythe in a heavy field. He dropped the scythe and, terrified, ran for the farmhouse, 'vaulting over fences like a hurdler'. Breen described the black snake as being ten feet long, with a body as thick as a man's thigh and 'eyes bright as a lantern'. His yells for help alerted others and the Sproulls thought he had gone mad until Breen calmed down and told them about the enormous snake.

Nicholas Sproull and his son got their guns and went out to the cornfield. Not far from where the Irishman had dropped his scythe, they killed a black snake as thick as a broom handle. Breen laughed when they showed it to them and insisted that the dead snake was merely one of the big one's babies. Breen went back to Ireland, where there are no snakes to frighten excitable farmhands.

❧❧❧

A mahogany log that was sawn through in Belfast in March 1908 was found to contain a clearly defined image or 'photograph' of a small deer and a larger animal running. The report concluded that the 'photograph' had probably been transmitted by lightning during a storm and the picture must have been taken a long time earlier because the tree, which was four feet in diameter, was an 'exceedingly old one'. Every board cut from the log clearly showed the image.

❧❧❧

In May 1908 a boy from Buncrana, County Donegal swallowed a toy balloon, which had a whistle attached to it. It lodged in his throat in such a way that every time he breathed he whistled. It could not be extracted by surgeons, but the obstruction was unexpectedly got rid of when the boy took a fit of coughing.

❧❧❧

An Irishman once saved the life of Queen Victoria near Kensington Palace in 1821, when the future monarch was only two years old. A soldier named Moloney was walking near the carriage in which the infant princess was being driven. When the carriage was overturned in a freak accident, Moloney rushed to the child's rescue and brought her safely out of the smashed vehicle. He broke his leg during the rescue and sustained other injuries from which he suffered for some time afterwards. The Duchess of Kent, the child's mother, gave him the munificent reward of £1 for his heroic act.

A few years later he was sent out to India with his regiment and remained there for over twenty years, before returning to England to retire, settling at Hounslow on a pension of sixpence a day. Being in poverty and distress, Moloney wrote to the queen, reminding her of the important service he had once performed for her. There was no reply. Undaunted, the old soldier wrote again, and continued to do so for nearly twenty years. At last a small donation came through the post anonymously. The following week it was repeated.

On the introduction of postal orders Moloney received one for £1 almost every week from the same nameless benefactor. As the orders all bore the Windsor postmark, the old veteran suspected the source. One day a slip of paper which seemed to have been put into the letter accidentally revealed the name of the sender. The money came from Sir Henry Ponsonby, the queen's private secretary. Moloney continued to receive the £1 weekly until his death at the age of eighty.

Moloney was originally intended for the Church, but being a wild youth, he left home at an early age, taking with him a large sum of money belonging to his father. He soon spent this, then enlisted in the army as a necessity. Moloney was well educated and had an especially wide knowledge of the classics. He used to amuse his fellow soldiers by quoting verses from the Latin and Greek poets.

❧❧❧

The arrival of the mysterious Turk Dr Achmet Borumborad in Dublin in the late eighteenth century caused a sensation. Who he was and where he was from no one could guess, although everyone from the highest society circles to the lowliest street urchins had their own opinion. The doctor cut a very striking figure in the city. He was the first Turk who had ever walked the streets dressed in his colourful native garb and speaking fluent English.

The sight of the tall Turkish man sporting a rich black beard and wearing an immense turban was a seven-day wonder. Dr Borumborad had a talent for making friends and quickly became a fixture on the social circuit. His standing in the community was further enhanced when it became known that he intended to set up the city's first public baths – to be based on the Turkish baths in his homeland – which were badly needed at the time.

The good doctor proposed to offer the public 'Hot and Cold Sea-water Bath' and free medical consultations to all. He had little trouble finding patrons willing to back this worthy scheme and the Irish parliament quickly voted him the necessary funds. The baths proved very popular with rich and poor alike and provided Dr Borumborad with a good living. Year after year fresh funds were voted for the baths as a matter of course.

Before every parliamentary session Dr Borumborad held lavish dinner parties for his wealthy and influential patrons. During one of these evening matters got out of hand and several drunken grandees accidentally fell into one of the baths. They became a laughing stock, and the doctor lost many of his patrons after the unfortunate incident. For some time Dr Borumborad had been seeing a Miss Hartigan, who had agreed to marry him provided he shave off his beard and convert to Christianity.

He promised to do this, but she refused to see him again until he kept his word. That same evening a gentleman arrived with a message from the doctor. When Miss Hartigan agreed to see him, in walked a very fine looking well-dressed man she did not recognise. She was further taken back when he got down on his knees, seized her hand and started kissing it. 'Don't be angry, my dear creature!' the stranger cried out before she had a chance to gather her wits. 'To tell the honest truth, I am as good a Christian as the Archbishop; I'm your countryman, sure enough! Mr Patrick Joyce from Kilkenny county, the devil a Turk any more than yourself, my sweet angel!'

She was astonished, but this did not stop Miss Hartigan from keeping her word, and the couple lived happily ever after. Unfortunately, the baths did not survive long when their proprietor's true identity became known, and they were subsequently closed down.

❧❧

Spectators at steeplechases in the early 1800s had a sure way of ensuring that their favourites won the race – they cheated, resorting to any tactics to ensure the desired outcome. Forewarned of the danger that he might be pulled off his horse or pelted by stones, Englishman George Smith decided to risk competing in a steeplechase across the Limerick countryside in 1833. Smith came up with a clever strategy to outwit the locals. Setting off on his horse Fidler, wearing his jockey's colours, Smith stopped and put on an overcoat and hat, before spurring his horse into the lead. As he approached the fences where the locals lay in wait he shouted at them to make way as the favourite, who was in the lead, was just approaching. Believing that Smith was another spectator following the race, they let him through without any harm or injury and he raced to victory.

❦❦❦

William McFadzean from Lurgan, County Armagh was awarded the prestigious Victoria Cross for a selfless act of heroism during World War I. McFadzean was a 20-year-old infantryman in the British Army's 14th Battalion, Royal Irish Rifles. On 1 July 1916, during the Battle of the Somme near Thiepval Wood, France, McFadzean was in a trench preparing for an attack. As he was opening a box of hand grenades for distribution, the box slipped down into the trench, which was crowded with men, and two of the safety pins fell out. McFadzean, instantly realising the danger to his comrades, courageously threw himself on top of the box of grenades, which exploded, blowing him to pieces. Only one other man was injured. Without a moment's hesitation the young Armagh man had given his life for his comrades. McFadzean's father was presented with his son's Victoria Cross by King George V in Buckingham Palace in 1917. It is currently on display at the Royal Ulster Rifles Museum in Belfast.

❦❦❦

Eagle Island is located off the coast of Mayo and is exposed to the full force of the Atlantic. Two lighthouses commenced operation on the Island in 1835, one on the west and the other on the east, 130 yards away. The lighthouses were built 133 feet above sea level on the rocky island, and the towers were another 87 feet high. Due to its exposed location the island is constantly struck by severe storms and being perched high above the sea did not prevent the lighthouses feeling the full fury of the sea. On the night of 17 January 1836 the lantern of the west tower was struck by a rock shattering one of the panes of glass and putting the light out, but the keepers had the light working again in an hour.

At midday on 11 March 1861 a huge wave struck the light room of the east tower more than 220 feet above sea level. It smashed 23 panes, washing some of the lamps down the stairs, and damaged the reflectors beyond repair. The light was restored the following night with a reduced number of lamps and reflectors. So much water cascaded down the tower it was impossible for the keepers to open the door of the tower; they had to drill holes in the door to let the water out. On several occasions the keepers' dwellings were badly damaged by storms. By the end of the nineteenth century the families were housed nearby on the mainland, while only the keepers remained resident. In 1895 the east tower was decommissioned and reduced in height, while new lighting was installed in the west tower. This lighthouse was finally made automatic in 1988 and no keepers have been resident on the island since.

❧☙

During the famine, when theft was rife in the countryside, a cottager from Coolcarney near Ballina, County Mayo was caught in the act of sheep-stealing one night and transported to Australia for his crime in 1847. It had been hoped that his capture would put an end the theft of sheep in the area, but it continued apace. Although no thief was caught, it was suspected that the convict's wife was the culprit and she was closely watched. When the watchers heard a suspicious noise nearby one night they investigated and found a sheep missing. It could only have been killed and taken by the woman.

They searched her house straight away, but found nothing. The watchers were puzzled and searched it again, with the same result. They men left and talked over what they had seen and heard in the cottage and decided to make a third search as they were certain the missing sheep was there. This time they found the dead sheep. It was in bed with the children, dressed in a nightgown and chemise. The law was not resorted to, but the woman and her young family were expelled from the locality and her cottage was knocked down.

❧❧❧

On 11 March 1760 the trading ship *Good Intent* from Waterford, bound for Bilboa, was captured by a French privateer off Ushant Island off the north-west tip of France. The ship had a dozen hands aboard and a cargo of brandy and iron. The privateers transferred most of the crew to their own ship, leaving five men and a boy under the command of nine Frenchmen to bring the ship to their home port in France.

Undaunted by the odds facing them, the remaining crew plotted to retake the *Good Intent*. Led by an 'intrepid' sailor named Brien, the Irishmen struck back when the privateers least expected it. Three days after being captured they chose their moment and acted. Four of the Frenchmen were below deck, three more were aloft in the rigging, and the last two were at the helm.

Brien surprised the helmsman, tripping him up and grabbing the man's sword and pistol. At the same time he shouted to his shipmates below to follow his example. Brien fired the pistol at the other man, but missed and flung it at the man's head, hitting him hard. The helmsman's arm was badly cut when he tried to defend his head from a blow from Brien. Below deck the other Irishmen attacked the four Frenchman and got their swords, compelling them to surrender. They were then shut below deck.

The remaining privateers surrendered and yielded the ship to Brien and his companions. When the privateers were safely locked below deck the victorious crew were now faced with another pressing situation. None of them could read or write or knew how to navigate to find their way to a friendly port. Brien had a fair idea of the course needed and took charge. He made a calculated guess and steered the *Good Intent* a few points off north. The following day the first land they made was near Youghal in Cork. The sailors happily made port there and lodged their prisoners in the town's jail.

⁂

A race took place at Ballyshannon, County Donegal on 3 November 1792. Four horses started for a sweepstakes of a hundred guineas. 'One of the horses was only to carry a feather and was rode by a boy. The first from the post was the horse carrying the feather. When he came to the wall he was stopped by the boy who, with great dexterity, alighted, turned the horse over, climbed the wall himself to the other side, mounted again, and came in first to the winning post. Another horse and his rider leapt clearly over, and the two other horses baulked at the wall. It is now contended that the horse rode by the boy has lost, because the latter dismounted at the wall.' The case was referred to the Irish Turf Club to be decided. A short while later they judged in the boy's favour, reasoning that 'there being a saddle on the horse's back when he leapt the wall, it was sufficient as a featherweight.'

⁂

William Douglas, Earl of March (1725–1809) was one of the greatest gamblers of his day, and he was not known for honesty when wagers were made. In 1751 the earl raced his horse Bajazet against Sir Ralph Gore's Black-and-all-Black at the Curragh racecourse in Kildare for a reported stake of 10,000 guineas. Bajazet was beaten despite his jockey managing to throw off some lead weights along the way in an effort to gain the day. This underhanded ploy was spotted by Gore and he demanded satisfaction, calling out March for a duel. The Scottish nobleman turned up the following morning at the appointed time and place. He was met by the sight of a polished oak coffin with a plate on its lid. On it was engraved March's own name and title, with the date of his demise, that same day. The sight unnerved March and he immediately apologised to Gore for his behaviour.

❦❧

George Nixon kept a hardware shop in Cork in the late eighteenth century. He began to notice that a lot of items had been stolen, but could not catch the thief. After a glass case where he kept buckles and other sundry items was broken into on the night of 5 February 1777, Nixon decided to set a trap for the thief, who would no doubt brazenly return to steal more items. The storekeeper obtained a 'rat gin trap', laid a pair of buckles on it as bait and placed the device in the case among other items. (The way a gin trap worked was that when a rat or other animal stepped on the iron plate in the centre, the metal jaws sprang shut, trapping the creature and badly injuring its leg. These traps were banned in the 1950s because of the suffering caused to animals.) The thief returned to the shop and tried to steal the buckles, but instead sprang the trap and caught his fingers in it. He was captured and brought before a magistrate, who committed him to jail pending trial. Once safely locked up (and no sooner) his fingers were released from the gin trap. He was later sentenced to be publicly whipped.

❧❧❧

An excursion boat, the *General Slocum*, caught fire on New York City's East River on 15 June 1904. It was the worst maritime disaster in the city's history, and an estimated 1,021 of the 1,342 people on board died. The crew tried to run the ship ashore at nearby North Brother Island, but the *General Slocum* got stuck on a sand bank offshore. Many people jumped overboard into the river.

Staff from the isolation hospital on the island heroically went to work, without thought of their own danger, and brought many people ashore. Two Irish women were foremost amongst the rescuers. Cork-born Nellie O'Donnell (1881–1929), an assistant matron at the hospital, was the first person into the water, despite the fact that she could not swim – she had often remarked to friends that she wished she knew how to swim. But when she saw hundreds of people about to drown she jumped into the river without any thought for her own safety. To her later amazement, though she thought nothing of it at the time, when she got into deep water she found she could swim. She grabbed a small boy by the collar and towed him back to shore. Then she went back again and again until she was exhausted. In all she brought ten people to safety. Afterwards she would take no credit for her unselfish act, saying that it was a miracle. She did say that she would never again dare venture into water over her depth after what she had seen and heard that tragic day.

Mary McCann, who was 17 at the time, was a patient at the isolation hospital. She had only arrived in the United States from Ireland a month earlier. At Ellis Island she had been diagnosed with scarlet fever and sent to North Brother Island to recover. She too plunged into the water and is also credited with saving ten children.

❧☙☙❧

English-born Francis James Shaw died at his home in Queensland, Australia in his 86th year. The first ship he embarked on at Liverpool in 1841 was stranded on the Welsh coast during a heavy fog. A few days later Shaw took passage in another ship bound for Melbourne with over two hundred people on board. In the Irish Channel the ship encountered a terrible storm and was driven on to the Irish coast in the dead of night. By the aid of a flash of lightning Shaw two sailors making their way along the mainmast yard arm, intending to jump onto the rocks on shore, and decided to follow their example. He climbed the rigging and made his way along the yard arm to join the sailors. Very soon the yard arm swayed over the ledge of the cliff and he and the sailors jumped to safety. No sooner had they jumped than the ship's masts and rigging collapsed like a pack of cards and every soul remaining on board the ship perished. Undeterred by his luck with ships Shaw ventured for a third time on the ocean a few weeks later. This time the voyage was uneventful and he finally reached Australia.

❧❧❧

One Thursday morning in 1927 a small boy from Fivemiletown, County Tyrone came down with a high fever. By afternoon his temperature had reached 105 degrees. The next day his temperature subsided. But exactly one week later, the fever returned, ran its one-day course, then subsided. Week after week the boy developed a burning fever each Thursday morning that rose to 104 or 105 degrees before the day was over. For the rest of the week his temperature was normal. Newspapers ran the curious story of the 'Thursday-fever boy'. The cause of the strange disorder remained a mystery until a Belfast pathologist studied a drop of the boy's blood under a high-powered microscope and was able to pinpoint the solution of the baffling mystery. A few weeks before his first attack of fever, the boy had been bitten on the foot by a rat caught in a trap. From this bite the boy had developed a rare disease known as rat-bite fever.

❧❧❧

A bizarre accident took place on a farm at Newlands, near Naas, County Kildare in May 1902. An old man named John Reilly bled to death after accidentally stabbing himself in the leg with a pitchfork. The Kildare County Coroner Dr Kenna held an inquest at the farm the following day. After the jury had been sworn in they were conducted to view the body, which lay in a loft over a cattle byre. The floor was very shaky one, and as soon as the twelfth juryman put his foot on it the entire structure gave way, pitching the doctor and jurymen down into the cattle below.

The only part of the floor that did not give way was where the body lay. Although the men only fell a distance of seven feet the byre was very dark and the cattle were naturally frightened at the sudden collapse. It was feared that some of the men may have suffered serious injuries, but beyond a few bumps and bruises suffered while struggling among the cattle there were no severe injuries. It was reported that the noise and confusion in the byre before the police opened the door and freed the men was indescribable. The cattle were bellowing, frantic with fright, while the men were shouting and swearing and bumping into each other or rolling around the mucky shed floor. When they were brought out the men were a very sorry sight. They were mostly covered from head to toe in cattle dung and all were in a foul humour. After a considerable time the inquest proceeded.

❧❧❧

Two fishermen from Ringsend, Dublin, James Hodgens and George Roden, were fishing in a trawler in Dublin Bay some six miles east of Howth in December 1891 when they made a macabre find. When they pulled in their fishing net they discovered that it contained the body of a man. When the remains were pulled into the trawler the men examined the corpse. George Roden identified it as the body of his brother, who had also been a fisherman and who had been drowned in the bay on 14 December 1890.

❦❦❦

In the *Philosophical Transactions* of August 1741, the Bishop of Clogher records an unusual encounter with a 70-year-old man from Innishannon, County Cork. 'Out of gratitude for a charity he had given him,' this elderly man 'shewed him a curiosity, which was that of his breasts, with which he affirmed, he had once given suck to a child of his own. His wife, he said, died when the child was about two months old. The child crying exceedingly while it was in bed with him, he gave it his breast to suck, only with an expectation to keep it quiet. But he found that the child, in time, extracted milk; and he affirmed, that he had milk enough afterwards to rear the child. His breasts were very large for a man, and his nipple larger than is common in women.'

❦❦❦

Irishman Lieutenant-Colonel W.L. Newell was at Sandown in April 1930, watching the Royal Artillery Gold Cup. This was a chase run over three miles and 125 yards. With only two to jump, one of the two remaining horses left in the race, Porphyrion, came down, throwing off its rider, E.B. Skey. Newell knew the horse well, having finished second on it at a chase at Newbury the previous year. 'I ran from the Tattersall's Ring Stand with Bobby Petre (a Grand National winning rider). The gateman let us out and we caught him before the winning post. I had on a good Donegal tweed suit and bowler hat, with umbrella,' Newell later said. 'Bobby threw me up and I rode back. Evan Skey was on his feet and running; but Max Tyler on a remounted Phillippa was now in sight, so he waved – "Go in"; I turned at the last fence and a mounted policeman tried to stop me but we eluded him and were over. It is a long ride in at Sandown through the crowd. We drew the weight and earned £50 for a second place, which was a lot of money when pay was only £18 a month.'

❦❦❦

The steamship *Metropolis* bound for Brazil with over 250 people aboard and 500 tons of iron cargo was wrecked on Currituck Beach, North Carolina, on 21 January 1878. Foremost among the heroes of the shipwreck was 34-year-old Timothy O'Brien from County Limerick. He was described in reports as being five feet six inches tall, 'very stoutly built, a Hercules in strength, and of the greatest physical endurance'. The *Metropolis* was the second wreck the Limerick man had escaped. The first was the steamer *Golden Gate*, which was lost off Acapulco in 1863. She had burned down to the water's edge, and the young Irishman was one of the 25 survivors who managed to swim ashore over a distance of seven miles. Soon after the *Metropolis* had struck and begun to break up there was a general rush for the rigging. O'Brien secured a spot high up on the mainmast, but soon realised his only chance of survival was to swim ashore. He dived off the mast and struck for shore, which he reached safely, the fifth survivor to do so.

Witnessing the peril of the other shipwreck victims in the sea, O'Brien ran to the Currituck clubhouse, three-quarters of a mile away, and got matches and materials to start fires. Dashing back to the beach he started several fires and dived back into the sea to rescue other survivors. One by one he brought exhausted and in some cases half-dead victims ashore to the fires. O'Brien didn't stop until five o'clock that evening, when the last survivor had been rescued.

In the seven hours he had saved nearly fifty people, many of whom would have perished without his intervention. The most remarkable rescue he made was that of Anne Huet, the only woman to survive the wreck. She was struggling in the breakers, supported only by a life-preserver, but clearly exhausted and about to drown, when O'Brien saw her and called to a young man named John Doherty to help him save her. The two men plunged into the surf towards her. Twice she was pulled from O'Brien's grasp by the treacherous waves, but he seized Anne at last and with Doherty's help brought her ashore unconscious.

She was barely alive and subjected to the crude remedy of being rolled over a barrel to get the salt water out of her. Then, still unconscious but breathing, she was gently laid beside one of O'Brien's fires. Thirty minutes later she came to and found her husband at her side. He had washed ashore forty yards down the beach. His first exclamation after being rescued had been 'Is my wife drowned?'

❧❧❧

On 26 September 1812 a bizarre foot race took place in Belfast in front of a large crowd. The race, for a wager of twenty guineas, was between a 70-year-old man who would be carrying a youth weighing 10 stone 7lb, and a young man. The two men had to race around the Linen Hall, a distance of a quarter of a mile. The older man had to make a circuit once, while the young man had to do it twice. Although encumbered by his piggyback rider, the older man covered the distance in four minutes, beating his opponent by a few yards. Betting on the event was at first even, but about halfway through the race it went three to two in favour of the older man.

❧❧❧

The terrible fate of being pressed to death by heavy weight remained as a punishment under law until the late 1700s. Any person on trial for a crime could be 'pressed to death' for refusing to plead.

At the Kilkenny Assizes in 1740, one Matthew Ryan was tried for highway robbery. When caught he had pretended to be a lunatic. In jail he threw away all his clothes and could not be made put them on again. Indeed, he went naked into the court for his trial. He pretended to be mute and would not plead. The judges empanelled a jury to try 'whether he was mute and lunatic by the hand of God, or wilfully so'. The jury returned in a short time, and brought in a verdict of 'Wilful and affected dumbness and lunacy'. The judges tried to persuade Ryan to plead, but he still pretended to be oblivious to all around him.

The law now called for the punishment of *peine forte et dure*, but the judges compassionately delayed passing this horrible sentence in the hope that the foolish criminal might come to his senses. But Ryan continued to refuse to plead and the judges had no choice but to pass sentence, ordering that he be pressed to death. The sentence was carried out two days later in Kilkenny's public market place. As the heavy weights were being piled on the wretches' chest, he begged the sheriff to hang him instead. But it was too late. The sheriff could not deviate from the prescribed punishment.

❧❧❧

When Lord Rawdon was in South Carolina during the American War of Independence in 1781, he had to send a vital message through a countryside teeming with the enemy. Corporal Dennis O'Lavery of the 17th Light Dragoons was chosen, for his courage and intelligence, to accompany the despatch rider. They had not gone far when they were attacked. The messenger was killed and O'Lavery wounded. He took the despatch and rode on until he fell from the saddle from loss of blood. Fearing that the despatch would be taken by the enemy he thrust it into his wound to hide it. O'Lavery was found the next day, at the point of death, by a British patrol. With his last breath he pointed to the wound. A surgeon later declared that the wound itself had not been fatal, but had been rendered so when he stuffed the despatch into it. Corporal O'Lavery was from Moira in County Down and his commander and fellow-countryman Lord Rawdon was said to have erected a monument to his memory.

❧❧❧

During the Seven Years War a force of some six hundred French troops under the command of the privateer François Thurot landed at Carrickfergus, County Antrim and captured the town and castle. The invaders occupied the town from 21 to 26 February 1760, only departing when a large force of local militia and a Royal Navy squadron approached. During the initial fight to capture the town an incident occurred that reflected well on one French soldier's humanity. As the defenders were fighting the attacking French force in the streets, a child escaped from a nearby house and ran in between the combatants. One of the French soldiers saw the child's precarious position, downed his weapon, grabbed the child and put it safely back in the house it came from. Then he resumed fighting.

❧❧❧

In his book *Shooting's Strangest Days*, Tom Quinn relates the curious tale of a clever bird, dating from 1877. During that year a boy was out shooting in summertime. He was near a freshly cut hay meadow and had shot some rabbits, when he saw a bright brown bird and lifted his gun to fire. Remembering that he had not reloaded, the boy chased the bird, which was running across the field. Moments later he saw the bird keel over. The boy picked up the seemingly lifeless bird and brought it home. His mother took the bird from him and laid it on the kitchen table, saying it was a corncrake. He did not tell her it had simply dropped dead, afraid he would not be believed. Instead the boy admired his catch as his mother pottered about the kitchen.

For a moment he thought the bird's eye opened and could not credit it. When it happened again he called out to his mother, but on hearing his voice the bird shut its eye again. Now both stood still and quietly watched the bird. A minute later its eye opened and the bird hopped off the table and ran out of the open door with the boy and his mother in close pursuit. Once outside it took to the air and flew away.

❧❧❧

Before the rebellion of 1641, Captain John Edgeworth, unaware of what was to come, left his wife and child at their home, Cranallagh Castle in County Longford. During his absence the rebels attacked and set fire to the castle. They dragged his wife out, literally naked, but she escaped and hid under a furze bush until they left. Then she fled to Dublin and on to the safety of her father's home in England.

The rebels plundered the castle, but were persuaded to put the fires out when they saw a portrait of the captain's mother. She was a Roman Catholic who had founded a religious house in Dublin and was a revered figure. The rebels found the couple's only child, a boy, lying in his cradle. One of the rebels grabbed the baby by the leg and was going to dash its brains out against the wall, when Bryan Ferral, a servant of the Edgeworths, stopped him, claiming the right of killing the 'little heretic' himself.

He swore that a quick death would be too quick for the baby and he planned to put the child in a bog hole up to its neck and leave it for the crows to pick its eyes out. He grabbed the child, ran with it to a neighbouring bog and thrust it in some mud. When the rebels had left, the man went back for the baby. He looked after the boy, hid him in a pannier under chickens and eggs, and carried him safely through the rebel camp and on to Dublin. The child was later reunited with his overjoyed parents.

❧❧❧

A startling escape from drowning after an accident occurred in Dublin on 29 November 1902. Philip Camrass, his wife, their newborn baby and a private nurse named Miss Harding took a cab, driven by James Ball, from their residence in Rathmines. They planned to catch a steamer for Glasgow departing from Alexandra Basin, and reached their destination well before six o'clock in the evening. It was dark and quite foggy, and the place was not well lit.

The driver, heading as he thought for the ship's side, drove over the quay into the water. There was some 25 feet of water in the basin at the time and the distance from the quay edge to the water was about 25 feet. Luckily the cab landed on the mooring rope of the steamer *Lady Olive* and was suspended between the water and the top of the quay wall. The horse, however, disappeared, carrying the shafts with it. It was thought that the unfortunate creature had drowned, but the horse had actually swum to the opposite side of the basin and got on shore. It was later found in a shipyard.

Meanwhile, the driver had been thrown into the water. His and the trapped passengers' cries attracted attention from people on shore and in the adjacent ships. James O'Malley, a watchman on the *City Of Caithness*, threw a lifebuoy to Ball, and started hauling him out, but the rope broke and he fell back into the water. O'Malley threw him a second rope and managed to pull Ball out this time. Meanwhile, the cab kept swaying on the rope, and the passengers trapped in the cab were in great danger. A plank was tied to a rope and on this improvised platform O'Malley was lowered down to the cab. He brought the passengers out through the window of the cab and they were hauled up to safety one by one. O'Malley was handed the baby first, and it nearly slipped out of the shawl it was wrapped in, but Philip Camrass caught it before it could plummet into the water. When all had been safely landed, the passengers wept with joy, and hugged and kissed the brave man who had run such a risk to save them. The cab remained balanced on the mooring rope until it was winched to the quay. The only injury was to Miss Harding, whose forehead was badly bruised. James Ball was taken to hospital suffering from shock, but the others went home, and the poor horse, whose knees were badly cut, was taken to Lambert's Livery Stables on Store Street for rest and treatment.

❧❧❧❧

The account of an unusual encounter with a strange boar-like animal was published in *Walker's Hibernian Magazine* in 1781. John Carrol was riding to Cashel from Tipperary on 19 December 1780 when he was startled by the roaring of a bull from a nearby stand of trees. At first he thought it was an animal belonging to a local farmer, but when the creature emerged from the trees Carrol could not believe his eyes. Instead of a raging bull, it looked like an ordinary-sized pig, but with one difference – 'it had spreading horns' growing out of its head.

The sight of this strange creature astonished Carrol, but after a moment he gathered his wits and urged his horse forward at a slow pace. The creature followed him for nearly a mile, and at a place called Thomastown Pool, Carrol was relieved to see it disappear into a cave at the side of the road. After its departure he rode on until he got home. The following night Carrol and four friends went to the cave, captured three of the same unusual animals and brought them home.

❧

The curious case of Longford-born Jane Bern came to light in 1790 when the Reverend Charles Perceval wrote an account of her to his doctor brother Robert. Her world was literally upside down. When the clergyman met the 11-year-old girl at the charter school she attended in Dunkerrin, County Offaly, he was struck by the curious nature of her eyesight. To read a book Jane turned it upside down and read upwards, from left to right. Her eyes moved perpendicularly, but she could not easily look upwards or see any object placed above her eyes. The unusual girl read perfectly, but could not write or perform such household tasks as knitting or spinning wool.

❧

A curious bankruptcy case lasted over a hundred years. On 23 May 1797, Robert Smith, described as 'a porter merchant' of Smock Alley in Dublin, was declared bankrupt after his business failed, owing the huge sum of £10,000. It was not until 1906 that Smith's creditors received a final settlement from the estate. Initially, creditors received only two shillings in the pound. Over time more money was brought into the porter merchant's estate and further monies were paid out in 1896 and 1900 to the representatives of the original creditors. These debts, amounting to about £4,400, were paid in full. A further sum of about £2,000 was discovered through the diligence of one of the creditor's solicitors and in 1906 the representatives who could be traced were paid nearly 20 shillings in the pound.

❧❦❧

The death of Bernard Gallagher, alias 'Willie John McGranaghan' in a Londonderry workhouse in June 1926 at the age of 70 marked the passing of a great hoaxer. Gallagher was a scamp and scoundrel, but a clever and ingenious one. He once hoaxed the Londonderry Harbour Board by taking a dry dock for the repair of a foreign vessel that never arrived. The story that a vessel was coming in for extensive repairs was widely circulated and many unemployed men thought they were going to get work.

On another occasion he marched up to a group of corporation workers and informed them he had the city surveyor's authority to fire them and hire a fresh gang in their place. Another time he posed as a government engineer sent to County Donegal to make a survey of a new boundary between the two states. Gallagher once bought several loads of hay and sent them to the Governor of Londonderry prison, a man with whom he frequently came into contact.

A Derry spirit merchant was once visited by a well-dressed seaman who claimed to be from the crew of a ship docked at the city. He handed in a large order on behalf of the ship's captain and asked the merchant to advance him half a sovereign and put it on the bill! In Omagh, Gallagher claimed to be 'Peter Doran', the long-lost father of a woman there. She believed him and put him up for a few days until he tried and failed to withdraw £20 from her daughter's bank account. A few days later he tried but failed to order dresses for his granddaughter from an Omagh shopkeeper. On an excursion to Buncrana, Gallagher claimed to be opening a mill there. In Derry he announced the opening of a quarry and hired a number of men, with picks and shovels, to start work.

In Coleraine, Gallagher acted as the representative of American businessmen and bought a parcel of land. The price was agreed, subject to confirmation from his American backers, and Gallagher was lavishly fed and watered for days while he waited for a reply. When it arrived, written, of course by himself, it was delivered by a boy hired by Gallagher (for sixpence). It said the money would arrive by the next mail, and the representative was to remain on the spot and sign the deeds.

Gallagher once acted as the Inspector-General of the Royal Irish Constabulary and inspected a barracks in a remote Donegal village. The inspection ended with Gallagher borrowing £7 from the head constable.

The hoax which first brought Gallagher to prominence and gave him the nickname that stuck to him was when he impersonated 'Willie John McGranaghan,' the long-lost son of a Derry family. On that occasion he was arrested and sentenced to five years in prison. No sooner than he was released he impersonated the long-lost husband of a Donegal woman. The deception was discovered when Gallagher removed his boots. The woman's husband had a toe missing, while Gallagher had all ten. This time the Derry conman was jailed for three years, with another five added on for being a habitual criminal. In court, he usually conducted his own defence quite skilfully. Gallagher had actually once earned an honest living as a barber, but it was said he 'shaved' many people over the course of his career of dishonesty.

❧❧

Veteran farmer James Prunty from Aughaward, Ballinalee, County Longford went into a shed housing a bull to clean it out on 21 January 1878. While he was working, the bull broke its restraining chain and attacked the 76-year-old. Prunty's daughter, Bridget, a deaf mute, happened to be passing by the shed and saw the animal cruelly attacking her father. Without hesitation she picked up a stick and beat the bull over the head, while grabbing the copper ring in its nose. The bull fought back, goring Bridget and knocking her against the wall, but she held on and continued to beat it with the stick.

At last the animal yielded and backed away. Bridget threw away the stick, and, changing her grasp of the ring to her right hand, picked up her badly injured father and carried him outside the shed, forcing the bull back and slamming the door in its face. Sadly, despite all her efforts, her father passed away an hour later. Poor James Prunty had been thrown around the shed by the bull and gored and stamped on and his injuries were too severe. Bridget's heroic actions were widely reported and praised.

During his tour of Ireland between 1776 and 1779 Arthur Young recorded seeing several gigantic ash trees. Most memorably, at Donirey, Clare Castle, County Galway, Young saw a small class of schoolchildren being taught in the hollow trunk of a living ash tree. It was 42 feet in circumference.

In 1751 a murder was solved by a dream. Adam Rogers, who kept a public house at Portlaw, County Waterford dreamed that he saw two men at a particular spot on a nearby mountain and that one murdered the other. One of the men was small and sickly, the other strong and large. The dream was so vivid that Rogers told his wife and several neighbours, including the local priest, about it. Some time afterwards Rogers was startled to see a pair resembling the men in his dream come into the public house.

He told his wife and they kept a close watch on the men. The small man, Hickey, was returning home a wealthy man to his family in Carrick after many years abroad. His companion was called John Caulfield. They had met on the way back to Ireland and became friends. The publican did not like the look of Caulfield and tried to persuade Hickey to stay, saying that he would accompany him to Carrick the following day, but Caulfield persuaded Hickey to continue on and Rogers could do nothing.

An hour after leaving Portlaw the men reached the same lonely part of the mountain Rogers had dreamed of and Caulfield murdered Hickey and stole his money. The body was still warm when it was discovered by locals a short time later. Hearing of the discovery of a body, Rogers and his wife went to the spot and identified the corpse. They were able to provide a good description of Caulfield and tell of their suspicions. Two days later he was arrested in Waterford while attempting to get passage on the first ship leaving port. At his trial Adam Rogers and his wife were the main witnesses against the accused man, but there was other testimony too: after killing Hickey, Caulfield had continued to Carrick, and doubled back towards Waterford by a back road. When his guide, a young boy, noticed blood on Caulfield's clothes, he was bribed to keep quiet.

The Rogers gave a detailed description and account of Hickey and Caulfield. They proved that he had taken a new pair of shoes that Hickey had been wearing and had put his old shoes on the corpse. Under cross examination Adam Rogers admitted that he had taken an unusual interest in the two strangers entering his premises and was forced to relate his foreboding dream. Witnesses including Rogers' local priest, who came forward to corroborate his testimony. Caulfield was found guilty of the murder and executed.

❧❧

Patrick O'Bryan from Loughrea, County Galway had the distinction of being hanged twice. As a young man he enlisted in the Coldstream Guards, then deserted after finding a soldier's life too dull for his liking. The rakish Irishman lived a lavish lifestyle, ran up debts and took to thievery, then highway robbery to support himself. He led a short but furious life, before finally being caught, found guilty, and hanged at Gloucester. After hanging for the prescribed amount of time, his body was cut down and given to his friends for burial.

They were astonished, when they got him home, to find that there was still life in the highwayman. An able surgeon was hired to bleed O'Bryan and was able to revive the rogue for a fat fee. O'Bryan was much chastened by the experience – for a while. His resurrection was kept secret and plans were made to provide the Galway man with a fresh start. His friends hoped he would turn over a new leaf.

For a while O'Bryan lived an honest life, but when memory of the fate he had escaped faded, he stole a fresh horse and took to highway robbery again. A year after his execution he held up the man who had prosecuted him. The unfortunate man could not believe his eyes. After toying with his prey, O'Bryan shot him in the head and hacked the body to pieces with his sword. On another occasion he led a gang who broke into the house of a wealthy Wiltshire gentleman. The gang brutally raped the man's daughter, then stabbed her and her parents, tied up the servants and set fire to the house, burning it to the ground. They made £2,500 from this robbery alone.

O'Bryan remained at liberty for another two years, until one of his accomplices was caught and confessed his crimes on the gallows, implicating the Galway man. After a while O'Bryan was tracked down and caught. This time the authorities made sure to hang him properly. After the execution his body was taken down, boiled in tar and hung in chains near the spot where he had murdered the household in Wiltshire. He was 31 years old.

❧❧❧

Macquarie Island, several hundred miles south of New Zealand, is one of the most remote places in the world.

When Captain John King Davis visited the island aboard the *Nimrod* in May 1909, he was startled to see smoke coming from one of the sealers' huts, since he believed the island to be deserted. Davis sent a party to investigate. As they rowed ashore, a man and two small dogs walked to the shore to greet the boat. There was a heavy surf, but the Crusoe-like man pointed out the best landing place, walked into the water and helped the men drag the boat ashore.

The hermit was William McKibbin, from Carrick Island, Ballylongford, County Kerry, who had served in the Royal Navy for over twenty years. He had come to Macquarie to work as a sealer but when it came time to sail, McKibbin announced that he intended to remain on the island. He wanted to save enough money from sealing during the winter of 1909 to buy himself a boat when he returned to Hobart. Nothing the other sealers could say could persuade him to leave the isolated island.

When Captain Davis went ashore he was welcomed by McKibbin and escorted to the little hut where the Irishman lived with his two little dogs, Fido and Nell. Davis was deeply impressed by the hut, which was very warm and comfortable and had all the comforts of home. McKibbin presented him with a juicy pie and a loaf of bread fresh from the oven. Davis thought the pie, made from elephant seals' tongues and hearts, was 'excellent'. Along with the breasts and livers of penguins, this was the only meat the 51-year-old Irishman had, but he looked fit and healthy on this diet. McKibbin kept himself busy preparing the digesters for another season of work, and had also killed several elephant seals, building up a valuable store of oil and blubber for himself in the digester house.

When the weather was too bad for outside work he sat in the hut making mats and smoking. The digester house was a shed containing boilers where seals' blubber was rendered into oil and packed away into barrels for shipment.

No pressure from Captain Davis could induce McKibbin to return with him – the Irishman was happy where he was and had everything he needed. The veteran sailor remained on the island for another year after a ship failed to return for him and a party of nine fellow sealers until June 1910. By then food supplies had run perilously low and the men had to live off the land. Under McKibbin's leadership they survived by eating penguins, seals, small birds and anything else the island could provide. When their clothes wore out McKibbin made new ones from spare blankets. New boots were fashioned from tough strips of elephant seal hide. All the cooking, eating and sleeping had to be carried out in the miserable twelve foot square hut, which was quite an ordeal for the men. When their coal supply was exhausted they had to rely on timber from old shipwrecked boats. They lived off the island for four months until they were rescued and were understandably bitter after their unexpected ordeal. McKibbin earned enough to buy a small cutter and fished out of New Zealand for some time, but his ultimate fate is unknown.

❧❧

Prince was a very remarkable dog, half Irish terrier, half collie, from County Cork, who found his way alone from London to the trenches during World War I and was reunited with his master there. Private James Brown went to France with the 1st North Staffordshire Regiment in September 1914, leaving Prince with his wife in Buttevant, County Cork. She took Prince with her when she went to Hammersmith, London, to live, and one day he disappeared. After a fruitless search, she wrote to tell her husband the sad news. The following day she heard that Prince was with him in France, having turned up two weeks after disappearing. Brown was returning to his quarters near Armentières when a friend from his battalion called out to him: 'I've got your dog here, Jimmy.' Brown took it as a joke, but when he looked he found it was indeed Prince and the pair were delighted to be reunited.

The regiment adopted Prince as a mascot and he remained in France during the war. He was given a jacket made from an old khaki tunic and had his own identification disc. The dog became a great favourite with the men and amused them with his many tricks. Prince was a born ratter, once killing 137 rats in a day, which was greatly appreciated by the men in the trenches. Prince returned to England in May 1919 and by then he was famous. After going through quarantine the dog returned to live with his master. The dog's years of war service wore him out prematurely and he died on 18 July 1921. He was lying beside his kennel when he saw a mouse and gave chase. Prince caught it, but the exertion was too much for him. He crept away into a cellar and died. When his story was first told in the press many people refused to believe it, but the Royal Society for the Prevention of Cruelty to Animals investigated and proved its veracity.

❧❧❧❧

Londonderry-born Volney Beckner (1748–1760) was the son of a poor fisherman and had a tough but loving upbringing. His father could not afford to send him to school on a regular basis, so he educated Volney at home, and trained him from an early age for a seafaring life. While he was still only a baby his father taught him to be absolutely fearless in the water and to swim confidently, even in rough seas. Volney was often thrown from the stern of the boat and made to swim until he was exhausted. Then he would be pulled aboard.

This Spartan training stood to the boy. By the time he was four Volney could swim some three or four miles in the wake of his father's boat and only allowed himself to be hauled out of the water when he could swim no more. At the age of nine the boy was apprenticed aboard a merchant ship his father occasionally sailed. Volney proved to be a natural sailor and thrived under the tough conditions. He was utterly fearless; during stormy weather he would climb the mainmast and 'hang there as calmly as if lying in his hammock'.

By the age of 12 Volney had earned his fellow shipmates' respect, and the ship's captain saw fit to promote Volney and double his pay. 'I do not doubt,' he said in front of the entire crew, 'that if this little man continues to display so much valour and prudence, he will obtain a place very far above that which I now occupy.'

On one voyage to France Volney's father was on board, as were a number of passengers. A little girl fell overboard, and

Volney's father, who was nearby, heard her screams. With a shout to put the ship about he dived overboard to rescue the girl. He got to her just in time and started back for the ship. Suddenly he saw a shark swimming for them. Those on board saw it too and could only look on helplessly. Volney grabbed a sabre and leapt into the sea. Diving under water, he came up under the shark as it neared his father and the girl. The boy drove the sabre up to the hilt in the shark's belly.

Badly wounded, the shark broke off the attack and tried to get at Volney, who kept stabbing and hacking at the creature. It was a terrible sight. The sea was crimson with blood and the trio were struggling for the ship. By now they were close to the ship's side and ropes were thrown down to pull them to safety. Father and son each grabbed one and were hauled out of the water by their anxious shipmates. It seemed they were out of danger at last. They were still dangling a foot or two above the sea when the maddened shark shot out of the water 'like a rising salmon' and bit Volney in two with 'a hideous snap of teeth'. Part of his lifeless body was dragged on board. His father and the girl, who were pulled to safety, owed their lives to the heroism of the 12-year-old boy.

❦❦❦

Trial by battle was an ancient method of deciding law cases. Strange as it may seem, this barbaric remedy remained on the statue book until 1819, when it was finally repealed as the result of a celebrated English murder case in 1817. In 1815 a man named Clancy shot and killed one Brian O'Reilly in broad daylight near Mullingar, County Westmeath in front of several witnesses. Clancy was arrested and made a full confession. He was brought to trial at the Mullingar Summer Assizes the same year. As it was thought Clancy's confession was all the evidence required to convict him, the prosecution called no witnesses to testify. Through a technicality the confession was held inadmissible, and with no further time allowed to call any witnesses Clancy was acquitted. O'Reilly's brother appealed the decision and the matter remained in the courts for some time. After several adjournments Clancy offered to settle the matter by trial by battle with the dead man's brother, but following a compromise between the two parties the matter did not proceed. Under this deal Clancy withdrew his claim for trial by battle, pleaded guilty to the murder and was transported for life.

The Ranties were a tribe of diminutive people who until the 1850s lived in an area covering over 3,000 acres in the Glengarriff Hills in County Cork. They usually married within the tribe, saying that they were too busy to court, so they married women close at hand. They spoke a curious Irish dialect that outsiders found very hard to understand.

The Ranties farmed and fished and had little contact with the outside world, except when they occasionally brought coral sand and seaweed to Bantry in boats to sell to the local farmers. The women wore red cloaks which they dyed using a secret process known only to themselves. One story goes that when the French tried to land at Bantry Bay in 1798, they were startled by the sight of red-coated British soldiers waiting high up on the mountainside. In reality these were all the Ranties women Lord Bantry could muster high up on the side of Sugarloaf Mountain. The French delayed their landing, but were driven out of the bay by a storm. The Ranties were decimated by a cholera outbreak in 1832 and by the famine in 1848. Afterwards they started to marry outsiders and gradually they merged with the surrounding population. The last resting place of the Ranties is said to be the old graveyard of Killeenah. Their origins remain a mystery, but one story says that they originally came from Ulster in the sixteenth century.

❧❧❧

While cruising off the Cork coast in July 1893 the Royal Navy ship HMS *Apollo* narrowly avoided running aground on the rocky shoreline a few miles from Crookhaven. A thick fog had fallen and visibility was so poor that literally nothing could be seen off the ship's bows. The ship had been making for Castletownbere but had lost its way and was heading towards the coast at Toormore, five miles away from Crookhaven.

Two fishermen from Long Island, Schull, who were gathering carrageen moss on the rocks at Toormore, were surprised to hear the sounds of an approaching steamer. When the fog lifted for a moment the men were horrified to see a warship heading directly for them at high speed. At great risk to themselves the fishermen shouted and signalled to the oncoming ship, and about fifty yards from the shore the ship came to a halt. According to the two fishermen, Thomas Goggin and John Regan, the ship's captain leaned over the side of the warship and politely inquired, 'Is this Bantry Bay?' If the captain was surprised when Goggin and Regan informed him of his location, he did not show it. The fishermen offered to pilot the warship back to the safety of deep water and the captain gladly took them aboard to do so.

❧❧❧

Some Londonderry gentlemen played an amusing practical joke on a publican in the city in March 1864. They got a donkey and carefully sewed it up in a bullock's hide. At night one of them called to the public house, and offered to sell it to the publican, saying that he had been at Buncrana fair and had failed to sell the 'bullock' there. The publican looked over the animal in the darkness and started to bargain for it. So well was the donkey disguised in its 'new dress' that he had no inkling of the trick being played.

A good price was asked for the 'bullock', but, after a good deal of haggling the sum asked for was reduced to £2 10s. The animal was lodged in a outhouse overnight and left a feed of hay to eat. In the morning the publican was puzzled to see that it had not eaten any hay.

A closer inspection of the animal in daylight showed that its mouth had been sewed up to prevent it braying and giving away its identity. When the hide was cut, the donkey began to bray, leaving the publican in no doubt that he had been tricked. The publican stoically freed the unfortunate donkey from the bullock hide, and let it make itself comfortable in the shed. Rather than be publicly ridiculed he refused to pursue the hoaxers who had duped him. Instead he sold the donkey and hide – at a loss of £1.

❧❦❧

Passengers on the steamer *Princess Beara*, which sailed between Castletownbere and Bantry in Cork, had a frightening experience on 2 August 1909. The Royal Navy cruiser *Sutlej* was conducting gun-firing practice anchored off Glengarriff when the steamer, heading for Bantry, unwittingly sailed between the battleship and its target out at sea. Three live six-inch shells were fired in quick succession and struck the water close to the steamer. The passengers were terrified and huddled on deck, expecting to be blown to pieces. One shell hit the water fifty feet astern of the ship, exploding a huge column of water. Another passed over the ship and dropped into the sea two hundred yards on the other side. Aware of its mistake, the cruiser ceased firing, allowing the *Princess Beara* to sail on to Bantry.

❦❧

The great polymath George Petrie (1790–1866) lived at No. 21 Great Charles Street, Dublin. He loved animals and kept several. When a kitten belonging to his favourite cat broke its leg one night, Petrie was greatly upset and rushed out to get one of his friends, who was a surgeon, but could not find him. Petrie tried another surgeon, and had hardly knocked on the man's door when the strangeness of his quest struck him. He was about to leave, but thought it best to wait to apologise for calling. The door was opening and Petrie was forced to enter and wait in the study while a servant got the surgeon out of bed.

In a few minutes the surgeon came down, carrying his boots, and assured Petrie that no apologies were necessary. The surgeon put on his hat and cloak on and accompanied him home, where Petrie worked up the courage to tell the nature of the case. The surgeon good-naturedly answered, 'Well, let me see the patient at all events.' He was shown the kitten and carefully put its leg in a splint and bandaged it up. The surgeon refused any money and promised to call the next day to see his patient.

As Petrie went to show the surgeon out, the kitten's mother, who had watched proceedings, sprang up on the table and retrieved the kitten and carried her offspring to her bed. To Petrie's amazement she proceeded to undo all the surgeon's bandages, 'deliberately taking out pin by pin', and removed the splints. Then she started to lick the broken leg and continued to do so for same days and nights, hardly stopping for a moment. The kitten's leg healed perfectly.

❦❧

The schooner *Cymric* of Arklow, County Wicklow once collided with a tram. The unique incident occurred on 28 November 1921 at Victoria drawbridge in Ringsend. The bridge operator decided to allow the tram to cross the bridge and signalled this to the schooner, but she was suddenly blown forward by a gust of wind and her bowsprit speared the lower saloon of the passing tram. A window was broken, but there were no injuries.

Another ship collided with the same bridge some years later. The *Happy Harry* from Arklow had intended to glide under the open Victoria drawbridge on 20 December 1943, but for some reason it went off course and managed to ram and get stuck in the open bridge. It was peak morning rush hour and it took half an hour to remove the ship, allowing the bridge to be lowered and the frustrated commuter traffic let through.

❧❧❧

D r Dobbs, a physician in Youghal, County Cork, enjoyed walking on the strand. One morning he passed by a cottage where a large number of people had gathered to mourn the passing of a woman who had died the day before. Dr Dobbs walked on some distance, but became uneasy, wondering if the person about to be buried was actually still alive. The doctor hastened back to the cottage and found the coffin, closed up, under a large table, around which family and friends of the deceased were sitting drinking to her memory.

Dr Dobbs expressed his uneasiness that the woman might not be dead, and asked to examine the body. Some mourners thought he was joking; others became angry and insisted that the corpse would be interred as planned. The doctor had to threaten them with the law if they moved the body without his permission. This threat had the desired effect and he was allowed to examine the corpse. When the coffin was opened Dr Dobbs quickly realised that the woman was still alive.

The poor woman was removed from the coffin and put into a warm bed. In a short while she began to show clear signs of life. The doctor attended the woman for several hours until he was satisfied with her recovery. In a few days the woman visited the doctor to thank him for saving her from an awful fate. She offered him a fee, but the doctor refused to accept it. The woman was quite put out at this, but was able to persuade him to accept some small token of gratitude in payment for his kindness. Dr Dobbs agreed to accept a pair of knitted woollen gloves (as he knew she was a good knitter), and both parties were satisfied. For a great many years afterwards the woman presented the doctor with a fine pair of woollen gloves on the anniversary of the date of her deliverance.

❦❦❦

In June 1734 Captain George Walker of the *Eliza* was anchored off Cadiz, Spain. On board was a friend of his, an Irish physician named Burnet, who was going to take passage on the ship back to Ireland. The two men were close companions and would talk about everything and anything. One night the conversation turned to the supernatural. The captain was a sceptic and did not believe in ghosts, but Burnet did, and was ridiculed by his friend. The doctor decided to see how far his rational friend might waver in his conviction.

Next day Burnet, an excellent swimmer, bet his friend he could swim underwater from the ship to some boats in the distance and startle the occupants with his unexpected appearance. Walker agreed to the wager and Burnet stripped off and dived overboard. All aboard crowded forward to the side, eagerly expecting the doctor to pop out of the water at the boats. Their excitement turned to shock when he failed to emerge. It seemed Burnet had drowned and all were horrified.

In fact, Burnet had dived under the *Eliza*, come up on the other side of the ship and climbed up a ship's ladder into the captain's cabin. He put on one of Walker's nightgowns and hid all day in a closet in the room. That night, Walker, deeply saddened by his friend's death, was lying in bed unable to sleep when he saw the closet door open and a human figure in white step out. In the moonlight it looked like a ghost. At first Walker thought it was his imagination playing tricks and turned away. When he looked back the figure was slowly advancing. He recognised his dead friend and called out, 'What are you?'

The first mate slept behind a division at the back of the cabin and heard the captain call out. He was not yet in bed and came running with a candle in his hand. When he caught sight of Burnet, he collapsed to the ground from the shock. Now seeing that his joke had gone too far, Burnet came clean to Walker and went to the mate's aid. He brought the man round with smelling salts, but the mate fainted again on seeing him. Walker took over his care and sent Burnet out of the room. The doctor roused the crew and explained his actions. The mate never got over the awful shock and was never the same man. He could not even bear to look at Burnet.

❧❧❧

Cannon Ball was a Connemara pony stallion that was famous all over Connemara for his unmatched speed and stamina, and he held an unbeaten record at local race meetings. When Cannon Ball died in March 1926, at the age of 22, his broken-hearted owner Harry O'Toole of Leam, Connemara, held a wake in his house for the pony. He had the body taken into a kitchen and laid out on an improvised bier. A half barrel of porter was placed in the corner of the room, and the pony was 'waked' as if it had been a human being. Shortly after midnight the body was placed on a large stable door, which had been taken off its hinges, and carried by ten men to a nearby grave lined with hay. There, in the dead of night, Cannon Ball was laid to rest, and a local poet recited the following verse over the graveside:

Sleep, brave old pony, thy race is run,
No more with earthly kin you'll mingle;
Dream of racecourse tracks you've won,
Of noble steeds and epic deeds,
And bookies left without a jingle.

❧❧❧

On his way home to Brackenstown near Swords, north Dublin on 7 September 1800, Alexander Manders stopped briefly to adjust his saddle. No sooner had he jumped off when two robbers with pistols appeared from nowhere and held him up. They took his money and fled at the sound of an approaching carriage. Three days later Manders was in Thomas Street in Dublin when he recognised the thieves. At the same time one of the men saw Manders and knew he had been spotted. This man, Farrell, pulled out a pistol, but before he had time to use it, Manders hit him in the face with his own pistol and knocked him down. The other thief, a man named Usher, meekly surrendered and was dragged to the nearest jail with Farrell. Watches, pistols and other valuables were found on the men.

❧❧❧❧

One Mr Ennis from Downpatrick, County Down had a narrow escape from death on the night of 23 November 1808. He owed his life to a pocket book he kept in his jacket. Ennis was stopped near Santry by two armed robbers, one holding a sword and the other a pistol. The weary traveller denied he had any money. 'We shall see,' said one robber, pointing the sword at Ennis, while the other man seized his horse and motioned him to dismount. As Ennis got down he rushed at the man with the pistol and knocked him down.

Ennis would have succeeded in wrestling the pistol from him if the other robber not wounded him in the arm with the sword. Ennis turned to him and parried another blow, but was badly cut. While he was distracted the other man hit Ennis on the head and stunned him. While he lay on the ground the swordsman stabbed him in the chest. Luckily the sword hit the pocket-book in Ennis's side pocket and stopped the sword running through him. The robbers rifled through his pockets and got away with a large sum of money.

❧❧❧❧

An unusual combat took place in the house of a Naul innkeeper in June 1820. A hen was wandering around a room followed by its sole remaining offspring when a rat ran out and seized the chick. As it was being dragged away the chick's shrieks brought the hen to its rescue. She flew at the rat, grabbed it by the neck and attacked it. In the space of a few minutes she killed the rodent, then went back to mothering her chick.

❦❦❦

A soldier named James Vesey was returning to Dublin from his estates in the south of the country on 15 February 1743 when he was held up by two highwaymen near Castleknock and robbed of £800. Two brothers, Martin and Sylvester Keogh from Rathcoole, were suspected of the robbery. The brothers had a 'sinister reputation' and were spending more money than they could have earned honestly from their six-acre farm. They were arrested and brought before a magistrate.

Vesey identified Martin as one of the men who had robbed him. Due to a lack of evidence his brother was released without charge, but Martin was found guilty and sentenced to death. The money was never recovered. Martin was taken to Kilmainham gaol to await execution. Vesey, whose leave of absence had been extended for the trial, hastened back to his regiment in England. Over time he rose to the rank of captain and served in many military campaigns. He fought at the Battle of Fontenoy on 11 May 1745 and was badly wounded and captured by the French.

Vesey made friends with a fellow Irishman who had fought with the enemy, Count de St Wootsan, and Vesey discovered his life had been saved by a private in the Count's regiment, who had rescued him from the battlefield and got him medical aid. Curious why this man, Martin Vaughan, had never made himself known to him, Vesey tracked him down and was shocked to find that his saviour was Martin Keogh. The two men became friends, but Martin would not say how he had cheated death. But years later, when the gaoler of Kilmainham had died, Keogh finally related how he had escaped.

Eager to get his hands on the stolen money, the gaoler had offered to smuggle Martin out of jail. Martin's brother Sylvester gave him all the money, and Martin walked out of the gaol, while a corpse was dug up and put in his cell. No one suspected he had escaped, but Martin fled to France and joined the army there. Keogh later retired from the army, married a Frenchwoman and settled in Paris, setting up a successful business. His name disappeared from the register of army pensioners in 1769. Vesey was later freed and continued in the British Army, rising to the rank of colonel. He died at Bath in 1776.

❧❧❧

Charles Smith's *Ancient and Present State of the County Of Down* (1744) contains an account of a remarkable individual who adapted to his disability and refused to let it hold him back in life. James Walker was born in Hillsborough in 1718. His birth was a difficult one due to the baby's awkward presentation in the womb, and Walker's mother was in labour for four days. The midwife could not manipulate the baby into a better position and called a doctor, John Sedgwick, who arrived to find the baby's arms protruding.

The midwife had been unable to put them back into a normal position and they had remained presented that way for two days. They had become very swollen from the 'contractive force' of the neck of the uterus. Dr Sedgwick saw immediately that it would be impossible to get the arms back into position. He called for the family clergyman and outlined the cold facts to him and the woman's husband.

Dr Sedgwick believed the only option that remained was to try and save the woman's life. It was impossible to deliver the child and it was most likely already dead. They agreed with him and the doctor amputated the baby's arms. With their removal he was able to manipulate the baby and deliver it feet first. Believing that the child was dead, Dr Sedgwick passed it to the midwife, who laid the infant aside. A moment or two later the baby boy cried out, to the surprise of all. Dr Sedgwick stitched up and dressed his wounds.

The baby grew up to be a fine man. At the age of 25 James Walker was described as six foot tall, 'slender and narrow shouldered, active and nimble'. He could mount a horse without any help, rode with great skill and fearlessness and could stay in the saddle for hours on end. Walker dealt in horses for a living and covered large distances buying and selling. He could dress and curry a horse 'as well as any groom', holding the curry comb between his chin and shoulder. He could also drive a plough and dig with a spade, but found this uncomfortable. Walker had incredible dexterity with his feet. He could pick up a stone with his foot and throw it with force and hit any target he wished.

❧❧❧

It is not often that ocean waves set cliffs on fire, but it is possible. In 1731, near Doon, Ballybunion, County Kerry, part of the steep cliff face fell into the sea and exposed a large deposit of sulphur pyrites and iron. The combined action of water and exposure to air oxidised the deposits and set the whole cliff aflame. The fire lasted for years, burning like a volcano and producing great heat and a steady sulphurous smoke with a foul stench. The fire ate into the cliff, destroying a huge chunk of it.

❧❧❧

William Thompson (1775–1833) was the son of a wealthy Cork merchant. As a young man he visited France and became a dedicated socialist. When his father died in 1818, Thompson returned home to the 2,000-acre family estate at Carhoogarrif, near Glandore. In 1829 he set up a model co-operative on the estate. Tenants were given allotments of between three and twenty acres and were provided with specially built houses. Thompson kept a close eye on the community and built a hundred-foot round tower on high ground overlooking the estate so that he could keep watch on it.

Thompson was clearly a man of many talents. He gave public demonstrations of chemical experiments, which led his tenants to believe he was a wizard. He pulled their teeth and treated their illnesses, although it is not recorded how successfully. He carried out numerous experiments in new farming techniques. Hearing that the flesh and bones of all animals contain the same ingredients as wood, Thompson fed his pigs on a diet of straw, peat and sawdust. The wealthy eccentric could often be seen strolling about with a French tricolour tied to the end of his walking stick. He was a teetotaller and non-smoker, and for the last two decades of his life was a vegetarian, declaring that he could read and write better without meat. The mainstays of his diet were bread, potatoes and turnips. Although he did not eat eggs or butter, he allowed himself two luxuries; tea, and honey from his own hives. Once a mouse got stuck in a hive, and Thompson licked it clean before releasing it.

When Thompson died in 1833, his family buried him in local Drombeg graveyard, despite the fact that he had hated all forms of organised religion. A few days later, when the eccentric's will was read, his body had to be dug up. Thompson had directed that his body was to be put on display 'to aid in conquering the foolish and frequently most mischievous prejudice against the public examination of corpses'. He had also instructed that his ribs were to be 'tipped with silver so that it might present a fashionable appearance'.

There is confusion about the fate of Thompson's skeleton. He had willed it to the first successful co-operative established in Britain or Ireland, but a Dr Donovan later claimed that he had been given the task of preparing the corpse on condition of 'stringing up the bones and sending them as a memento of love' to a close friend of Thompson's. She did not get the skull, though; it was left to a French phrenologist.

Thompson left his estate to the Co-operative Movement, but his family contested the will and the case dragged on for 25 years. Ultimately the family won, but by then there was little left, as lawyers for both sides had drained the estate.

❧❧❧

Belfast woman Elizabeth Carson loved travelling on luxury ocean liners so much that she crossed the Atlantic Ocean 250 times. For the greater part of thirty years Mrs Carson was a familiar figure to the crew and officers of the Cunard Line and customs officials on both sides of the Atlantic. She is said to have been very friendly with the Astors, the Vanderbilts and other wealthy families who met and befriended her on her many trips across the sea.

Her love of the sea began in 1864, shortly after the death of her husband, when Mrs Carson and her daughter crossed the Atlantic to visit her brother. They stayed with him and he left Mrs Carson a fortune of $500,000 when he died a few years later. This ample legacy enabled her to indulge her love of the sea. Leaving her daughter with friends, Mrs Carson took a trip to Belfast.

She returned a few weeks later, saw her daughter was in safe hands, and from that day until her death a month seldom passed that she did not take a voyage across the Atlantic. She never missed a trip of the *Lucania* after the liner was launched and held the officers and its master Captain McKay in high regard; so much so that in her will she left $50,000 to the captain and other amounts to the crew. After her daughter married in 1883 Mrs Carson was free to spend her entire time at sea. Her daughter and son-in-law tried to restrain her trips through legal means when it emerged that she had already spent $250,000 of her fortune. When Mrs Carson threatened to disinherit to couple they backed off and left her free to spend and travel. (Perhaps in revenge, she left only $1,000 to her daughter.) Mrs Carson died in 1897 at the age of 74, after falling ill from pneumonia on her last trip across the ocean.

❧❧❧

The celebrated diarist Jonah Barrington was surprised in March 1780 to receive a challenge to a duel from a man he had never met, but he was obliged by custom to accept it. Barrington knew the challenger, Richard Daly, by reputation but had never met him. Daly had fought sixteen duels in the previous three years – three with swords and thirteen with pistols. Remarkably, in each case, both Daly and his opponent had escaped serious injury. Barrington had no pistols, so he and his second, Richard Crosbie, spent the night before the duel constructing a pair from parts of old pistols.

When the duellists met on 20 March 1780, Daly's second approached Crosbie, apologised and asked to call off the duel as the challenge had been mistakenly offered. Barrington was in favour, but Crosbie refused. He took out a copy of the *Clonmel Rules*, a set of rules drawn up in Ireland in 1777 to govern the conduct of duelling. Crosbie pointed to rule No. 7 –'No apology can be received after the parties meet, without a fire.' The duel had to proceed and both men took their places and fired. Daly missed, but Barrington hit his opponent. Daly staggered, put his hand to his chest and cried, 'I'm hit, sir.'

Luckily, the ball had hit a brooch and had driven a broken piece into Daly's breastbone. Crosbie, a jack of all trades, took charge and tended to Daly, calmly removing the broken piece and dressing his wounds. When Barrington asked why Daly had issued the challenge, Daly's second, angered by Crosbie's strict adherence to the rules, had the satisfaction of having the last word. He pulled out his own copy of the *Clonmel Rules* and quoted No. 8 – 'If a party challenged accepts the challenge without asking the reason of it, the challenger is never bound to divulge it afterwards.'

❦❧❦

An RAF airplane flying over Lough Neagh on 18 May 1931 suddenly dived and crashed into the only boat in the whole area, killing one man. The incident occurred when RAF pilot William Sharpe was flying a bomber over the lake on a training exercise. It seems that Sharpe had been overly careless; he had been practising bombing dives and misjudged his height. In a later enquiry Sharpe claimed to be flying fifty feet above the lake, but eyewitnesses said his height was nearer twenty feet. On one dive the wheels of the bomber caught the slender mast of the only fishing boat in the area. It broke the mast, smashed an oar and ripped irons off the sides of the boat.

The aircraft then somersaulted and dived into the lake, lying there partially submerged and upside down. Sharpe was able to scramble out and get to safety, but the two men on the fifteen-foot boat he had hit were not so lucky. James Hannan and his 33-year-old son, also James, were out fishing. The elder James saw the aircraft coming in low and threw himself flat on the deck, shouting a warning to his son. But it was too late. By the time other fishing boats reached the Hannans they found the dying man in the arms of his father.

An enquiry found William Sharpe not guilty and acquitted him of all charges.

❧❦❧

A man was hanged by mistake in Waterford in 1835 and it was partly his own fault. In 1816 Waterford man Daniel Savage murdered his wife and fled. In 1834 a brother of the murdered woman was travelling in the south of Ireland and was horrified to see Savage approach. He stopped Savage and accused him of the murder. The man replied that he was sorry he had not killed more of them. He disappeared, but was later caught that December and jailed in Waterford city.

The man known as Daniel Savage went on trial at the Spring Assizes the following March. The prisoner was so sure of acquittal that no witnesses were called for the defence. Three witnesses for the prosecution were unable to identify the prisoner as Daniel Savage. The only one who did confirm his identity was a brother of the murdered woman. The jury, however, found Savage guilty and the sentence of death was passed. The brother who had sworn to his identity stated that there was a scar on Daniel Savage's cheek and the prisoner had a similar one.

Prior to his execution the prisoner was shaved, but no mark was found on him. After he had been sentenced the man continued to declare his innocence. Savage's sister received permission to visit the condemned man before the execution. When she saw him in the condemned cell, she turned back again, exclaiming that it was not her brother.

On the scaffold he was too nervous to speak before such a large crowd, but made the clergyman who attended him promise to prove his innocence. A week or two after the execution it was proved beyond doubt the executed man was not Daniel Savage. His name was Edmund Pine from Kilmichael, County Cork. He had never been married and had not known the murdered woman. Why had the man not proven his identity and defended himself?

From the reports of this awful injustice it is possible to conclude that Pine suffered from mental problems. When he was first arrested he confirmed his name was Daniel Savage and answered positively to every question put to him. He suffered from frequent fits, which 'had the effect of reducing him to the state of a simpleton or an idiot'. Questions were raised in the British Houses of Parliament about how the tragedy had occurred. The then Prime Minister, the famous Duke of Wellington, was forced to defend the authorities.

He said Pine had an attorney and counsellor to defend him, but the prisoner had remained doggedly silent on his identity and had made no effort to prove his innocence. The simple-minded Cork man fully believed he would be exonerated. From the moment he had been jailed he had made money selling some of his food to his fellow prisoners. With the money he saved Pine had planned to buy a spade and other farming implements on his release.

❦❦❦

Thomas Mathew of Thomastown Castle in County Tipperary was famous for his lavish hospitality. He was handsome, wealthy and well travelled, with a wide circle of friends. As a young man he decided to devote his energies entertaining his friends. Having inherited estates and an income of £10,000 he husbanded his fortune carefully and went to live abroad for seven years, living on £600 a year. With a sufficient nest egg saved, Mathew returned to Thomastown Castle and set about transforming it into a luxury hotel for his friends.

It had forty guest rooms and every luxury Mathew could think of was provided for his guests' entertainment. He recreated a city coffee house, where they could eat at any hour of the day, read newspapers and periodicals and play games such as chess and backgammon. An authentic tavern was also provided. For those who liked outdoor pursuits such as fishing or shooting, Mathew supplied all the equipment, and a large number of horses and two packs of hounds were also kept for those who hunted. The less energetic could enjoy the house gardens or walk in the grounds.

His guests were expected to make themselves at home and enjoy themselves. There were only two restrictions: gambling was not allowed; and the servants were not to be tipped. Although Thomastown provided lavish accommodation it was an extremely well-run undertaking. Mathew worked hard to keep the house running smoothly and through prudent planning and management he improved the estate, passing his fortune on intact to his heir.

One famous visitor to Thomastown Castle was Jonathan Swift. He was invited to stay for a fortnight by Thomas Sheridan, who knew Mathew. When Swift saw the size of the castle and heard there would be other guests, he was all for turning back, and had to be persuaded by Sheridan to continue. He gave in reluctantly, saying, 'Well, there is no remedy, I must submit, but I have lost a fortnight of my life.' At first Swift decided to eat alone in his room and avoid fellow guests, but four days later he ventured to join the others, announcing before dinner, 'And now, Ladies and Gentlemen, I am come to live among you and it will be no fault of mine if we do not pass our time pleasantly.' He clearly enjoyed his stay as he remained there for four months.

❧❧❧

James Spratt (1771–1853) from Harold's Cross in Dublin was a remarkable man. He was one of the heroes of the Battle of Trafalgar in 1805 and his exploits on that day read like fiction. The 35-year-old sailor was master's mate on the 74-gun HMS *Defiance*. During the battle the *Defiance* engaged the enemy ship *L'Aigle*. When cannon fire from the enemy ship petered out, Spratt, who trained and commanded his ship's sixty-strong boarding party, got permission from Captain Durham to board the enemy ship with his men.

As the ship's boats were shot through and useless, Spratt proposed to swim across – his men 'could swim like sharks'. He shouted, 'All you, my brave fellows, who can swim, follow me!' He jumped overboard, armed with a cutlass between his teeth and a tomahawk in his belt and swam to the stern of

L'Aigle, then climbed the rudder chain and entered her gun room. In the noise and confusion of battle, Spratt's men had not heard his orders and now he was alone on the ship, one man against several hundred.

He fought courageously through the different decks towards the poop deck, where his shipmates spotted him waving his hat on the point of his cutlass and cheering. By now the two ships were side by side and Spratt's men could board *L'Aigle* and rally to his support. Their arrival was timely for Spratt was attacked by three grenadiers with fixed bayonets.

In the melee Spratt killed two attackers and was grappling with the third when they fell to the main deck. His opponent was killed, but Spratt was uninjured. Meanwhile, the British sailors had the French on the back foot and they were retreating. One French officer found himself at the mercy of two attackers and threw himself at Spratt's feet begging for quarter. Spratt threw himself over the man's prone form and saved his life – officers could be used for exchange or ransom. The veteran sailor joined in the desperate hand-to-hand fight for the ship. One grenadier tried to run him through with his bayonet, but Spratt parried it with his cutlass. The Frenchman stepped back and levelled his musket at his chest. Spratt struck down with his cutlass and knocked the musket away, but it went off and the musket-ball struck just below the knee of his right leg, shattering both bones in his lower leg.

Two more sailors attacked him, but Spratt managed to get to the side of the ship between two guns and held them off while other boarders came to his rescue. A few moments later

Captain Durham saw Spratt on the side of the ship holding his bloody leg over the railing and heard him shout, 'Captain, poor Jack Spratt is done up at last.' Spratt was quickly slung on board the *Defiance* and brought to the surgeon. The boarders were repelled by the French a short while later and swam back to the *Defiance*.

Captain Durham hauled off and fired at the enemy ship until it surrendered half an hour later. The surgeon wanted to amputate Spratt's badly injured leg, but Spratt refused to let him. Captain Durham tried to persuade the injured sailor to allow the operation, but Spratt merely held out his other leg and said, 'Never! If I lose my leg, where shall I find a match for this?'

Spratt was hospitalised at Gibraltar for four months. He kept his leg, although it was now three inches shorter than the other, leaving him lame. For his heroic actions the Dublin man was promoted to lieutenant. After recovering, Spratt returned to England and took command of a signal station at Teignmouth, Devon, and found the time to invent the homograph, an early form of semaphore. He later commanded a prison hulk at Plymouth, before retiring from the Royal Navy in 1838 with the rank of commander. Spratt married and put down roots at Teignmouth, where he raised a large family. He was a familiar figure in Teignmouth, where he rode around on a small Dartmoor pony. Despite his handicap, he remained a skilled swimmer and saved lives on several occasions; and on his sixtieth birthday he swam fourteen miles for a wager.

❧❦❧

A dog saved a newborn baby who had been abandoned by its heartless mother on a farm at Benagh, near Newry, in April 1813. The infant had been placed in a pigsty at night and it was found alive the next morning surrounded by the pigs. By a miracle it was unharmed and this was due to the protection of the farmer's large mastiff. It had stood guard over the baby all night, 'keeping the voracious animals at a distance'. The child was rescued and baptised with the name John Benagh.

❧❦❧

Enniskillen-born James E. Liddy (1828–1921) is an unsung hero of history. James and his family emigrated to America in the 1840s and he later settled near Waterton, New York and became a blacksmith. During a shopping trip to Waterton with his wife in 1853 Liddy was inspired by the coil-spring cushion seat on the buggy that made the journey more comfortable. Liddy thought how much more pleasant it would be to sleep on springs.

At the time, beds consisted of a heavy mattress laid on cross ropes tied to a frame. Liddy experimented with his idea; he sawed several wooden slats, fixed them to his bed frame, fastened several coil springs to each slat and laid a mattress on top. The result was a far softer and better bed. Liddy never patented his idea and there is no evidence that he undertook manufacturing bedsprings, but his idea was certainly the genesis of a new industry and provided a more comfortable sleep for humankind.

❧❧❧

The Berners Street hoax was a famous event that occurred in London in 1810. Prankster Theodore Hook bet he could make any house in London the most talked-about address in a week. Hook sent out thousands of letters summoning a multitude of deliveries, tradespeople, professionals and dignitaries to the house on a certain date. The result was mayhem: the street was blocked all day and the police had to be called in to disperse the crowds. A reward was offered for the capture of those behind the hoax, but Hook was never brought to account.

Ireland had its own smaller-scale version of this famous hoax. A large number of tradespeople were instructed by letter to call at the home of General Rice at Sandycove, Dublin at 2 p.m. on 18 June 1888. They included wine merchants, undertakers, grocers, furniture removers and many others, and the scene was chaotic. General Rice had no idea why he had been targeted as he had never done any harm or injury to anyone.

❦❦❦

Simon McCone from Drogheda, County Louth and his shipmates had to resort to the desperate measure of cannibalism to survive when they lost their ship. McCone was a crewman on the ship *Mary*, which had picked up a cargo of three hundred slaves, beeswax and some ivory in West Africa in 1735. The ship sprang a leak on the journey to the West Indies and the crew fought hard to keep the ship pumped out. Exhausted by their efforts, they released some slaves to help with the pumping.

This worked for a few days, but with food and water running low and the leak getting worse, the crew knew the ship could not last long. On 8 November the slaves stopped pumping and revolted, grabbing all the food and liquor they could. In the confusion McCone and seven other men escaped to the ship's boat with several bottles of water and brandy and cast off, abandoning the slaves and the fifteen remaining crew members to their fate.

In the little boat were four Englishmen, two Portuguese, an American named Thomas Thompson and McCone. Their only option was to set a course for the West Indies some five or six hundred leagues (roughly two thousand miles) away.

Four weeks later the men were relieved to see a ship and raised a distress flag. Instead of rescuing them the ship took one look at the small boat crammed with starving men and sailed away, leaving them to their fate.

'Our hunger then being intolerable,' McCone later wrote, 'we were forc'd to kill one of our companions to eat, and so agreed together to begin with one of the Portuguese, whom we accordingly killed out of pure necessity, and cut his flesh in small pieces, dipt it in salt water, and hung it up to dry in the sun, until it was hard, and so eat it, tho' but very sparingly; and thus we were forc'd to do with four more of the crew out of the eight; we also killed the sixth man, but were forc'd so to do, because he would have killed me, for he struck me with the tiller of the boat, and had just bereav'd me of life, when this my comrade Thomas Thompson came to my relief, and we were forc'd therefore to kill him, tho' we flung him over board, for he was so rotten with the dry pox [lesions] that we could eat no part of him."

Now the sole survivors, McCone and Thompson, swore to stick together and chance their lives to fate. The starving men went for days with nothing to eat except for one small flying fish that flew into the boat, and some small barnacles they scraped off the boat's hull. On 19 January 1736 they were overjoyed to see land – the island of Barbados. They were too weak to row the boat to shore, but a ship from the island found them and set the men ashore at Bridgetown, where they swore a deposition as to the fate of their ship. Thompson died a short while later, but McCone survived.

❧❧❧❧

Fisherman Hugh Baker made an extraordinary deposition in Youghal court on 22 May 1623. Baker had been fishing in the mouth of Youghal harbour on 8 May when the notorious English pirate John Nutt captured him and put the Corkman to work on his ship. Baker testified that three hours after his capture the pirates took a bark belonging to Morgan Phillipps near Dungarvan harbour, where it had been driven after a chase.

Phillipps surrendered after Nutt had fired at his ship three times. Baker described how the pirates boarded the bark and looted it over several hours. They took a large sum of money from Phillipps, slaughtered a 'fat ox' that was on board, and stole a barrel of wine, 'some 40 or 50 yards of fine canvas, 5 or 6 rugs, some linen and woollen Irish cloth and two suits of clothes, a gown and a cloak which Phillipps wore. He wept at this complaining that the cloak had cost him £20.' There were fourteen women on board, twelve of whom were taken and 'ravished' by the pirates.

Nutt took one woman for himself and held her in his cabin for a week. The pirates captured another ship, off Land's End, taking belongings, jewellery and money to the value of nearly £400. Baker and a man taken from this second ship were able to escape one night while the pirates were drunk, by cutting loose a sea boat that was tied to Nutt's ship and sailing her to Kinsale. Baker was incredibly lucky to have made his escape after only a week's captivity.

Towards the end of the nineteenth century, Ernest Carleton Bass decided to become a bullfighter. Leaving his home in Ireland, he made for Spain, where he learned some swordfighting and bullfighting skills, then headed for the United States, where he worked as a vaudeville swordfighter. Bass drifted south to Mexico, where he fell in with the matador Don Manuel Cervera.

Billed as 'the American Matador', Bass proved to be a poor bullfighter. On his first appearance in Mexico City in 1903 Bass was so clumsy he almost eviscerated the bull and the crowd howled him out of the ring. Undeterred, the Irishman appeared in several more bullfights in Mexico before he lost his nerve and decided he could not face any more bulls. Bass and several other matadors, including Don Manuel Cervera, were scheduled to appear in St Louis, Missouri in June 1904, but the state governor stepped in to stop the bullfights going ahead, moments before the first was due to begin.

When the eight thousand-strong audience learned there would no refunds they rioted and set fire to the specially built arena, destroying it. A few days later Bass and the other unpaid bullfighters met with Cervera and accused him of withholding money he had obtained from the promoter. An argument followed and the furious Cervera pulled a knife and went for Bass. Cornered and afraid for his life, the Irishman pulled his revolver and fired, killing Cervera. A coroner's inquest found that Bass had acted in self-defence and he should not be charged with murder.

Following his acquittal Bass went on to perform in several bloodless bullfights. These involved tormenting the bull until it was extremely angry, causing it to charge and then dodging the animal. These fights were not a success and Ernest Carleton Bass disappeared from public view.

❦❦

A gang of pranksters caused mischief in Westport, County Mayo in December 1859. One night every door knocker in the town was stolen and left in a pile outside the home of Police Sergeant Flynn with a note saying that the writer had observed the untidy appearance of Flynn's front door, which he hoped would be painted and varnished forthwith to 'prevent the necessity of a stranger doing it for him'. As a small contribution the writer left a selection of various knockers of Westport, asking the sergeant to select one and return the rest to their owners.

Sergeant Flynn wisely took the hint. His door and that of the police barracks were immediately grained in imitation maple, and adorned with 'two of the handsomest knockers' in Westport. The remaining knockers were left at the barracks to be identified by their former owners. For a small fee, which was donated to a local asylum, the owners were allowed to regain possession of them. All unclaimed knockers were later sold at auction.

On 11 December the pranksters struck again. The town's police were lured some miles out of town and while they were gone a large eagle sculpture over the portico of the town's Eagle Hotel was painted bright red. Next morning scores of locals gathered to view the 'red eagle'. A reward was offered by the furious hotel owner for the discovery of the pranksters, but they were never found.

❦❦❦

Irish-born James Burns was well known in Nottinghamshire and the surrounding counties as a celebrated ventriloquist. Little is known about his background, but we do know that he married a woman from Shelford, Nottinghamshire, where they set up house. He made a living performing feats of ventriloquism at fairs, markets, races and other public events, but despite several lucrative offers he was never tempted to stray far from Shelford.

He usually carried in his pocket 'an ill-shaped doll with a broad face, wrapped in a piece of linen cloth', which he used in his act as a dummy. Numerous anecdotes relate his skill as a ventriloquist and his eccentric humour. He did go too far on one occasion in 1789, convincing a girl that she was hearing the voice of a child when there was none to be seen; the poor girl became so worked up she started having fits. Burns earned a short spell in prison for abusing his talents.

In March 1790 Burns was in a shop in Nottingham and threw his voice into a large canister on a shelf, convincing the staff that they had heard the sounds of a dying animal coming from inside it. They were about to search it when another customer pointed out the smiling ventriloquist.

In August 1792 the ventriloquist tricked a servant driving a wagon laden with hay into believing that he could hear a child's crying coming from the centre of the load. As the cries became louder and more frequent, Burns kindly offered to help unload the wagon to find the child. When most of the hay had been unloaded Burns took a fit of laughing at the man's simplicity and left him to load the wagon again.

On another occasion Burns was in a public house when he saw a servant girl preparing fish in the kitchen. She was just about to cut off the head of one of them when she heard it say, in a plaintive voice, 'Don't cut my head off!' The frightened girl threw down the knife and refused to prepare the fish.

Buying fish at a stall in Sheffield in September 1795, Burns asked the fish seller if the fish was fresh. She replied that it had been caught only the previous day. Burns doubted her claim and cheekily threw his voice into the fish. 'It is a damned lie, I have not been in the water this week, and you know it very well,' it cried out. The shocked woman admitted she had lied. Burns died at his home at Shelford in January 1796.

❧❧❧

Limerick once had its own version of the famous hanging gardens of Babylon. In 1808 wealthy Limerick banker William Roche built large stores, covering more than an acre of land, at the rear of the family banking business on O'Connell Street. On the roof of these stores Roche built his own private gardens.

The stores were constructed under a series of stone arches ranging from twenty-five to forty feet high. On top of these arches Roche built a series of terraced gardens. The side terraces measured 150 feet by 30 feet, the central terrace 180 feet by 40 feet, and the lower two 200 feet by 100 feet. On the top terrace were hothouses, conservatories and orangeries, heated by flues, in which were grown exotic fruits such as grapes, pineapples and peaches. This terrace was seventy feet above street level and commanded an incredible view of the city and surrounding countryside.

Vegetables and hardy fruit trees were grown on the middle terrace and flowers of every kind were cultivated on the lower terrace. Flights of steps led from one level to the next. The depth of earth in the gardens averaged about five feet, and the stores underneath were protected from damp by stone flags cemented together. An ingenious network of channels carried excess water through lead pipes concealed in the arches to the city drainage system. In dry weather the down pipes could be blocked to retain water and pump it back up to the garden surface. Rainwater that fell on the glasshouses was collected in cisterns. Manure was brought up from the ground by mechanical means. It was little wonder that these curious gardens fascinated so many people.

This incredible structure was built at a cost of £15,000; and the government rented the stores for an upfront payment of £10,000 and an annual rent of £300. The stores themselves were virtually indestructible. They were solid and fireproof and remained the same even temperature, so they were perfect for storing alcohol and other liquids. Roche's Bank managed to survive a national financial crisis in 1820, but by 1825 it was taken over and the family withdrew from the banking business. William Roche was a dedicated nationalist and became the city's first Catholic MP in 1832 after the repeal of the Penal Laws, holding his seat for three terms. After Roche's death in 1850 the wonderful gardens fell into decline and eventually the garden was removed and the structure partly demolished. Part of it still remains.

❧❧❧

Belfast-born Kenneth Mackenzie (1916–2009) famously brought down an enemy aircraft during the Battle of Britain by ramming it. On 7 October 1940, Mackenzie had already helped shoot down a Messerschmitt Bf 109 over London docks and then pursued another, firing at it until he ran out of ammunition. The enemy aircraft was hit but not fatally damaged and turned to head back to the safety of its base in France. Mackenzie pursued it and his quarry tried to evade him by diving almost to sea level.

Undaunted, the Belfast man closed in, positioned his Hurricane fighter on the enemy's port side with his starboard wing over its tailplane. He then slammed his wing tip hard down on the tail, which snapped off, sending the enemy diving into the sea. Mackenzie's unorthodox manoeuvre broke off the other part of his wing, but he was able to keep control. Despite being pursued by two enemy fighters and hindered by damage to his engine from enemy fire, the brave pilot managed to reach England and crash land in a field near Folkestone. This exploit earned him a Distinguished Flying Cross 'for skill and gallantry'.

Mackenzie managed to bring down at least seven enemy fighters during the Battle of Britain. He was shot down over Brittany in France in September 1941, but managed to ditch in the sea, scrambled into his dinghy and paddled ashore. He was later found and captured by a German patrol. He made a number of attempts to escape from prisoner-of-war camps, but all these were unsuccessful. Instead he feigned insanity so convincingly over a long period of time that the Germans repatriated him in October 1944. Once back in England Mackenzie began a new career as a flight instructor. After the war ended he remained with the RAF, serving around the world, and retired in 1967 with the rank of wing commander.

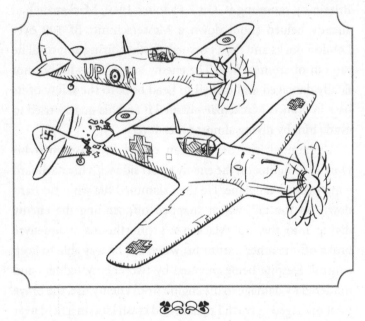

The Battle of Aughrim took place near the village of Aughrim, County Galway on 12 July 1691. The Jacobite army and that of the Williamites met there and a bloody battle followed. The losses on both sides were huge and an estimated seven thousand people were killed. Many of the dead remained unburied and were left on the battlefield for birds and beasts to feed on, including packs of fierce wild dogs; it became dangerous for anyone to be near the site on their own lest they fall prey to the dogs.

There is a remarkable story of a greyhound belonging to an Irish officer who had been killed. After the battle the body was stripped, but the dog remained with it night and day. Although he fed on the other corpses with the rest of the dogs he would not allow them or anyone else to go near his master's remains. When all the corpses had been eaten or had rotted away the other dogs left the battlefield, but the greyhound kept up his vigil. At night he would go to the local villages for food, then return to guard his master's bones. He remained there until the following January, when he went to attack a soldier who had gone too near the bones. Surprised by the sudden attack, the soldier unslung his gun and killed the poor dog with a single shot.

❦❦❦

James Boyle from Warrenpoint, County Down survived a terrible shipping accident near the entrance to Carlingford Lough on the night of 3 November 1916. Ninety-seven people died in the tragedy and 21-year-old Boyle, the sole survivor, could not swim!

Boyle was a fireman on board the coalship *Retriever*, captained by Patrick O'Neill from Kilkeel. The ship was heading for Newry with a full cargo. A gale force storm was blowing, making conditions extremely difficult. Boyle recalled that the ship had a slight list as the cargo of coal had shifted, but it remained under control. The steamship *Connemara* had just left Greenore port, heading for Holyhead in Wales with passengers and a cargo of cattle and sheep. The ships met in a narrow channel leading from Carlingford Lough to the open sea, and in the terrible weather conditions the *Retriever* accidentally rammed the *Connemara*, opening it from bow to amidships.

The steamer sank within minutes and the boilers exploded on contact with the sea. With her bows stove in, the *Retriever* fared little better, but she took longer to sink. Like the other ship, her boilers exploded when the sea water flooded them. Boyle was below deck when the accident occurred. He immediately went on deck and witnessed Captain O'Neill calmly order the crew to take to the boats.

Boyle jumped into one of the boats and drifted away. In the rough seas the boat overturned, but he managed to right it again. When it capsized again Boyle clung to the keel and held on for dear life. Half an hour after the ships collided the boat was driven onto the rocky shore near Cranfield Point and the exhausted survivor was rescued from the water by three local farmers who had heard the explosions. They took him to a nearby house where he was cared for until his family arrived to take him home. Boyle lived until 1967 but refused to discuss the tragedy until interviewed on television as an elderly man.

❧❧❧

Racing was banned by law in and around Dublin for some forty years as a direct result of the lawlessness of races held annually in the village of Crumlin. By 1789 the races became so intolerable to the inhabitants of Crumlin that they tried to prevent them going ahead, but to no avail; several days of racing brought the usual drunkenness and public disorder to the area. The following year the army was called in and the races were firmly stopped.

In 1791 a bill was introduced to prevent racing in the Dublin area. 'Whereas much idleness, drunkenness and riot have for some years past been occasioned by the frequency of horse races in the neighbourhood of the City of Dublin, for remedying whereof be it enacted ... that it shall not be lawful for any person to cause any horse, mare or gelding to run for any public prize whatever within nine miles of His Majesty's Castle Of Dublin.' This bill, which allowed racehorses to be confiscated and sold, remained in force until the 1830s.

❧❧❧

A tornado ripped through Limerick at 5.50 p.m. on 5 October 1851. Although it only lasted a few minutes it left a trail of destruction. The tornado cut across the city in a straight line from St John's Hospital to Sarsfield Bridge, causing huge damage to buildings and great destruction along its route, but a few feet either side of its wake the effects were hardly felt. Some residents nearby did not realise what had happened until the next day.

From a distance it looked like a column of dense smoke, and those close to it described it as having a roaring sound. When it hit the Shannon it produced a great fog, but the toll house keeper on Sarsfield Bridge could see small boats on the river lifted into the air. Two women crossing the bridge on a donkey cart were lifted out of the cart and blown across the bridge. One of them would have been carried over the parapet had she not caught a tight grip on one of the turned stone pillars that supported it.

Bizarrely, while the tornado stripped the slates off the domed roof of the Linen Hall, the model of a spinning wheel on top of the dome was undamaged. Two men were seriously injured when they were lifted thirty feet into the air. One of them was dashed against a wall and sustained multiple broken bones and a terrible head injury from which he later died. The other man was left in a 'precarious state', but survived. In the aftermath of the freak event three people were missing. Two of them were milkwomen, who were assumed to have been blown into the water. A man was said to have been lifted by the tornado and carried across the Shannon at a point where it was a quarter of a mile wide and deposited, unhurt, on the other side.

❦❧❦

Fights between women in armed and unarmed combat were very popular in Georgian London, because of their rarity. The Swiss traveller César de Saussure attended one of these gladiatorial matches in November 1725 and left an excellent description of an armed fight between an

Irishwoman and an Englishwoman. As in Roman times, the fight was held in a circular amphitheatre. As soon as the women entered the arena they saluted the audience, then each other. The women next 'engaged in a lively and amusing conversation', boasting of their strength and courage. One of them regretted she had not been born a man, otherwise she would have made a fortune through her skill. The other declared she beat her husband every morning to keep him in hand. Both women were scantily dressed, and wore little bodices and very short petticoats of white linen.

De Saussure described the Irishwoman as 'stout, strong and lithe' and the other woman as 'small, full of fire and agile'. They fought with two-handed swords with three-foot blades, the last six inches of which were sharp as a razor. The spectators bet large sums of money on the outcome. Stewards were on hand with long staves to separate the women if the contest got too bloody. When fighting commenced the women fought with the broadside of the sword, but did not hold back, 'and the combat became very animated'.

When the Irishwoman received a huge cut to her forehead the contest was paused. The Englishwoman's backers threw her money and applauded her, while the wounded woman's forehead was sewn up on the stage. The Irishwoman drank a 'good big glass of spirits to revive her courage' and the fight began again. This time each combatant held a dagger in her left hand to ward off the blows. The Irishwoman was wounded again and the contest was stopped to sew up her injury.

When the battle commenced for the third time the women held wicker shields to defend themselves. This time the Irishwoman received a deep wound to her throat and neck. The surgeon sewed it up, but she was too badly injured to fight on and her opponent was declared the winner. She received a few coins as a consolation, but the victor earned a good sum from the combat.

❦❦❦

While travelling with his mother on the Dublin to Wexford train on 24 October 1902, a four-year-old boy fell against the compartment door and was flung out when the train was travelling at full speed. The accident happened near Greystones and the alarm was raised at once. The train was stopped and a group of passengers went back up the line to pick up the body – they presumed he could not have survived the fall.

They found him alive and unharmed, except for a few cuts to the back of his head and forehead. He was brought to the nearest station and a doctor was summoned. The doctor found very little wrong with the little boy, and he and his mother were able to continue their journey home to Camolin, County Wexford on the next train a few hours later.

❦❦❦

Near the end of the nineteenth century a daredevil female cyclist attempted to ride along the parapet of the famous Spectacle Bridge, near Lisdoonvarna, County Clare. She failed and fell some thirty-five feet, but escaped unharmed except for some bruising, while the bicycle was smashed. At the same bridge, on 14 July 1904, a horse drawing a cartload of turf took fright, ran towards the bridge and jumped over it. The cart was prevented going over by the stonework, but the horse broke its traces and fell below. Strange to say, it escaped without any injury. It was thought that its fall may have been broken by trees or bushes.

❦❦❦

Thomas Johnson was an incredibly skilled horseman and trick rider. In the mid-eighteenth century he was famous to London audiences as the 'Irish Tartar', performing daring feats of horsemanship in front of paying crowds. Johnson burst onto the scene with his novel performances in 1758 and entertained large numbers of people with his skills in a field adjoining the Three Hats in Upper Street, Islington. First he galloped round the field standing on one horse. Then he went around again at full speed standing on two horses abreast with a foot on each animal.

Afterwards he galloped around the field with three horses abreast, shifting from one to the other. A reporter described another feat: 'While he was standing on the outside horse of the three, with all the reins and whip in one hand, he threw up his cap several times in the air, and caught it again, with the other, while the horses were in full speed.' At one time Johnson's act included riding on a single horse while standing on his head, but this trick 'gave pain to the spectators,' so he was obliged to discontinue it.

On being asked how he had learned his skills Johnson replied that 'it came to him naturally, for he learnt it by eleven years' practice.' Johnson earned a small fortune from his shows and continued to perform equestrian feats throughout the 1760s. Several prints exist of him 'standing on one, two and three horses in full speed'.

❧❧❧

When the 52nd Regiment of the British Army gathered at Arruda in 1810 to shadow the French forces under Marshal Masséna as they retreated, a peculiar adventure took place. An Irishman named Tobin in a company commanded by Lieutenant James Love went missing one night after being placed on sentry duty. Love knew the man well and, believing that he had been either killed or captured, reported him missing.

A few days later, when the regiment was on the march, Tobin rejoined his company, telling Love that he had been 'on a visit to the French General'. He explained that it had been the custom for the French and British sentries to meet at a wine-house halfway between the lines. One night he drank too much and fell asleep. A new French patrol, unfamiliar with the arrangement, took Tobin prisoner. The Irishman told them that he was a deserter, which gave him a better chance of escaping, and he had taken the opportunity to do so as soon as he could.

Some time later, an Irishman, who was aide de camp to Marshal Masséna, came to the British lines under a flag of truce to deliver some letters to their commander. At an outpost he met Lieutenant Love and, seeing his regimental insignia, asked about Tobin. He explained that Tobin had been brought before Masséna as a deserter. When the Marshal questioned him about the strength of the Light Division, Tobin offhandedly replied that it was ten thousand strong. When the French commander became angry with his reply,

Tobin asked what was wrong. The aide de camp explained that Masséna knew he was lying – the Light Division had four thousand men at most. Tobin told him to attack with ten thousand men, 'and if they don't lick him, I'm damned'. The Marshal laughed at his reply and offered to make Tobin a sergeant if he joined his force. The Irishman asked for a day to consider, and having made friends with a cook, filled his haversack, and took leave of the French in the night.

❧❧❧

A young Irishman living in Bristol met with a freak accident in 26 May 1856. Twenty-three-year-old Patrick Haggarty was relaxing with friends and neighbours when he ran after 'a buxom girl, who was engaged in seamstress work' and playfully gave her a hug. It proved to be a terrible idea; a needle the girl had pinned on the bodice of her dress impaled Haggarty in the heart and broke off, leaving nearly three-quarters of an inch in his body. The unfortunate man immediately felt ill and was taken to an infirmary. A surgeon carried out a delicate operation to remove the needle fragment with a forceps. Initially it appeared that the operation was a success, but Haggarty developed pneumonia and died a week later.

❧❧❧

A nnie McNally from Sligo heroically rescued seven children on 1 August 1907. She had gone with a friend and their children to bathe at Sligo Bay. As the tide was fast coming in they quickly returned to shore. Suddenly the women heard shouts for help and saw seven children standing on a little island that was completely submerged at high tide. The children had been caught by the tide, which had cut them off from the mainland, trapping them on the tidal island.

Although she could not swim, Mrs McNally rushed into the water to try and rescue the children. The island lay a quarter of a mile from the shore and several times Mrs McNally was almost overcome by the strength of the incoming tide. Her progress was also hindered by the fact that the ground was coated with a slimy mud. Eventually she reached the island and now she only had to save herself and the children! Taking the two smaller children in her arms and ordering the others to cling to her, the brave woman began her struggle back to dry land. The rapidly rising tide made it impossible to return the way she had come, so she took a longer route and miraculously reached the shore safely with all the children. The heroic Sligo woman later received awards from the Royal Humane Society and the Liverpool Shipwreck and Humane Society for her incredible act of bravery.

❧❦❧

Liverpool man Henry John Staff came to Ireland for a short visit in 1894. On 10 July he went on an outing to the Hill of Howth in north Dublin, and enjoyed a pleasant walk. At a spot between the Nose of Howth and the Bailey some pretty wild flowers caught his eye. He recklessly went down a steep slope near a cliff edge to pick them, but slipped and fell over the precipice. He was knocked unconscious by the fall. When Staff awoke three hours after the accident it was 9 p.m. and he was startled to discover that he had fallen on a rocky ledge about a foot wide.

Although he had been incredibly lucky, his position was extremely precarious. Two hundred feet above him towered the steep cliffs he had fallen over, and a hundred and fifty feet below lay the sea – and certain death if he slipped off the tiny ledge. Staff shouted for help, but there was no one around to hear his cries. Night came on and the poor man could only wait out the night in terror.

In the morning two Howth fishermen hauling lobster pots out at sea heard Staff's cries for help and spotted him on the cliff face. When they neared the cliff they saw that it would be impossible to rescue him, so they went to alert the police and coastguard. When a rescue party returned to save Staff it was apparent how awkward a location he was in. It was impossible to climb down and rescue him; instead, a rescuer climbed up from the sea and attached a rope that had been lowered down from the clifftop around Staff. When the exhausted man was firmly secured he was carefully lowered into a boat below and brought to Howth.

The descent was not without drama. During the rescue one of the coastguards had a narrow escape when a large rock fall just missed him. Staff was badly bruised from his fall, but, apart from shock and exposure, had no other injuries. The previous year another walker had slipped and fallen to their death on the same side of Howth.

❧❦❧

On the night of 19 February 1910 the Larne and Stranraer express mail train left Belfast with about thirty passengers. It reached Carrickfergus on schedule and was travelling at about fifty miles an hour when it passed a spot known as Briggs Loop, between Carrickfergus and Whitehead. At this point the rails ran close to an embankment which had slipped the year before. Since that time a watchman had been on duty at this point, and railway engineers had inspected the area a few days earlier and had discovered nothing to cause alarm. Heavy rains throughout the day had loosened the earth and a large landslide fell on the track just before the train reached the spot – another train had passed through safely just minutes before. The express comprised an engine, two mail vans, a guard's van, and four passenger coaches. In the darkness it ploughed into the landslide, which covered the engine right up to the firebox. The two mail cars were pulled through the landslide.

The collision derailed the passenger coaches and the last three were flung over the embankment, which was about twelve feet high, towards the sea. Thankfully the couplings held, preventing the carriages falling into the water. The passengers were got out quickly, little the worse for their adventure. All were suffering from shock, but there were no serious injuries, and no fatalities. The one man who could not escape immediately was a soldier named Lieutenant Wade, who was pinned in his carriage under a heavy piece of timber. It took rescuers a good half hour's work with axes and saws to release him.

One of the passengers, Mr Steele, graphically described his experiences. 'I was awakened by being flung against the opposite side of the carriage. I was bumped back again, but managed to open the carriage door, and the next thing I knew was being flung out on to some disused planks at the side of the permanent way. I was almost stunned. We rescued several women, including one lady who was holding a child.' Belfast schoolteacher Miss Walker had a terrifying experience. When her carriage was overturned she was thrown onto the roof, and as the water flooded into the carriage she had to climb to safety. By the time she was rescued, the water had reached her waist. She said 'it was an experience that she would not forget as long as she lived.'

❧❧❧

Irish-born Brian G. Hughes (1849–1924) was a wealthy businessman and famous practical joker. One of Hughes's most famous jokes involved a stray cat he bought in 1895. He carefully cleaned and groomed the animal and entered it in the first National Cat Show, held in New York. Hughes concocted an elaborate pedigree for the alley cat and gave it the name Nicodemus.

At the show Nicodemus was placed on display on a silk cushion inside a gold-plated cage and cared for by a female attendant dressed in a nurse's uniform. A florist delivered flowers daily and a uniformed servant showed up every day to feed the cat with ice cream and chicken. The pampered cat was a sensation, and attracted huge interest. Hughes received offers of thousands of dollars for his pet but refused to sell it. Nicodemus took a $50 prize for brown and dark grey tom cats. Ironically, Hughes later discovered his cat was a female when she gave birth to two kittens.

A few years later he pulled the same trick with a horse. A few months before the 1900 National Horse Show the prankster bought an old streetcar mare and sent it to his farm in upstate New York. There Hughes's head stable man spent a lot of time getting the horse into condition to compete. It was entered in the show under the name of 'Puldeka Orphan, by Metropolitan, dam, Electricity'. The hoax was discovered when one of the judges realised the name of the horse could be read, 'Pulled a car often, by Metropolitan, Damn electricity.'

On another occasion Hughes claimed to have funded an expedition to South America to capture a rare animal called a reetsa. For a while Hughes regularly updated the media on the expedition's progress, then announced the animal's capture. He organised a ship to pull into the docks on the Hudson River before the assembled press, who were astonished to see that the rare animal was in fact a steer (reetsa spelled backwards).

Hughes is said to have been the first person to drop fake diamonds in front of Tiffany's jewellery store. He hired an actor to play the part of a wealthy but clumsy dignitary, and watched greedy crowds scramble for the 'diamonds'. This prank was later used by the Marx brothers in a film. Hughes once placed picture frames and tools in front of the Metropolitan Museum of Art, which led to a search for apparently stolen paintings. On another occasion he offered to donate a plot of land to New York City to be used as a park. It turned out to be a twelve by eight foot plot of ground in Brooklyn. The incorrigible joker's favourite prank was to leave umbrellas in public places on rainy days. When someone took one and opened it a sign would drop down that said 'Stolen from Brian G. Hughes, New York'.

❦❦❦

Leitrim-born Charles 'Mountain Charley' McKiernan (1825–1892) led an adventurous life and is famous for surviving a horrifying grizzly bear attack. As a quartermaster in the British Army he saw service in Australia and New Zealand, later heading for California when word of the gold strike of 1848 reached 'down under'. He worked in the mines for a year before setting up a mule train business delivering supplies to the mines. This was initially very successful, but McKiernan later lost everything but his life when Indians attacked and took everything. Leaving the goldfields, McKiernan settled in the Santa Cruz mountains in 1850 and eked out a living farming and hunting game.

In the 1850s grizzly bears were widespread in the area and were hunted relentlessly. They could outrun a man, grew to around a thousand pounds, and were treated with a great deal of respect. It usually took several shots to kill one. Bear hunters favoured firing from an uphill spot and always had a horse nearby for a quick getaway. On 8 May McKiernan and a friend named Taylor started out for a gulch a mile away from his homestead where Taylor was planning to settle. After shooting a couple of deer the men spotted a female grizzly with two cubs. They decided to go for the bear and headed up the gulch to approach the animal from above. When they reached their chosen spot there was no sign of the bear and cubs. They followed a deer trail and unexpectedly came upon the bear waiting for them round a bend.

The grizzly was standing facing McKiernan at a distance of no more than six feet, her forepaws outstretched for a raking hug. McKiernan jammed the muzzle of his gun against the bear's chest and fired, while Taylor fired over McKiernan's head into the bear's face. McKiernan went to club the bear with his gun stock, but she beat down the weapon and seized him in her powerful forepaws. She crushed the front of McKiernan's skull in her jaws, before tossing him aside like a doll, and turning to Taylor. Meanwhile Taylor's small dog had attacked the two cubs. This distracted the grizzly, giving Taylor a chance to escape while she hunted the dog away. Taylor scrambled to the ridge top, believing that his friend had been killed instantly. The bear returned to McKiernan and dragged him to the end of a clearing.

After pawing him over in curiosity she left him and disappeared with her cubs. Taylor reloaded his gun and returned to the scene to find McKiernan alive and sitting up, but in shock. The attack had only taken a few seconds and he had remained conscious throughout. Taylor bound up McKiernan's head with his shirt and, leaving him his rifle for protection, went to bring a horse to carry the wounded man home.

A doctor hammered a silver plate out of two Mexican dollars and fitted it into McKiernan's skull where the bear had chewed away the bone over his left eye to the top of the frontal bone. Within three weeks the plate had started to corrode and was replaced with another one. McKiernan faced this ordeal without any anaesthetics. He suffered from terrible headaches for two years until a specialist removed the second plate and found a lock of hair underneath it. Fortunately this operation took place under anaesthesia. The bear attack left McKiernan terribly disfigured. He wore a hat low over his left eye for the rest of his life to hide this. Apart from this the brave Leitrim man enjoyed excellent health until 1890, when he became ill with a stomach complaint. He died in 1892, thirty-eight years after the bear fight that made him famous.

❧❧❧❧

Monaghan-born James MacLean (1724–1750) was known as the 'Gentleman Highwayman' as a result of his polite behaviour during his robberies. MacLean was from a good background and was well educated. His father was a minister, as was his brother, and MacLean was brought up to make a respectable living. His father died when MacLean was 18 and he squandered his inheritance in Dublin on high living; but his gentlemanly appearance helped him get a job as a servant to an Irish nobleman.

He was soon dismissed for making too free with his master's cellar, but not before getting a loan to buy a place in the army. Instead he spent this money on high living. He moved to London to hunt for a rich wife and found one in an innkeeper's daughter. MacLean settled down and kept a grocery for three years until his wife died. He sold the business and decided to use the money to find and marry a wealthy woman who would enable him to keep up the appearance of a wealthy gentleman.

With his money fast running out, an equally desperate apothecary friend named Plunkett suggested they take to the road as highwaymen. Despite a poor start to the partnership – MacLean fled from the first robbery, leaving Plunkett to carry it out by himself – the pair enjoyed a short but highly successful career as highwaymen, wearing Venetian masks to rob travellers around London. They always treated the people they robbed very politely and were never violent, although once MacLean's pistol accidentally went off and the ball grazed the skin under the writer Horace Walpole's eye. In a six-month period the gentleman highwaymen were said to have committed twenty highway robberies. The proceeds of these crimes allowed the men to live the high life.

MacLean was finally caught when he went to sell a fine waistcoat he had taken during a robbery. Unfortunately the dealer he had approached had originally sold it to MacLean's victim and recognised it. The highwayman was arrested and his apartment searched. A large hoard of valuables from recent robberies was found, alongside MacLean's large wardrobe of clothes and a 'famous kept mistress'.

Such was his reputation that his trial at the Old Bailey was a social occasion and nearly three thousand visitors came to his cell in Newgate prison on the first Sunday after his conviction. MacLean was condemned to death and executed on 3 October 1750. His companion in crime, Plunkett, was never captured.

❧❧❧

A train was travelling from Banbridge, County Down to Scarva, County Antrim on 8 April 1859 when the engine driver saw two men lying on the line between the rails. He immediately reversed the engine, but was not able to stop the train in time and it drove over the men. It finally stopped some distance beyond where the men lay. Railwaymen on the train went back to look for the remains; but instead of corpses they found the two men, alive and unhurt, but so drunk they were unconscious and oblivious to their narrow escape from death.

🏵️🏵️

While patrolling a coastal road near the coastguard station at Ballincarrig, County Wicklow on 23 July 1861, Constable Moon and another policeman spotted a dark object some distance away on the cliffs. Approaching it, they saw it was a young lad, about sixteen years old, lying fast asleep on the edge of the cliff. Fifty feet below, sharp rocks lay at the base of the cliff. Moon had no time to wonder how the boy came to fall asleep at this perilous location. He knew that waking the youth suddenly would be risky, 'So, with bated breath and beating heart,' he quietly approached the sleeper and firmly grasped him by the collar of his coat.

The boy awoke suddenly and, startled by the sight of two policeman, panicked, trying to get up and fighting the men's grip and nearly sending all three over the edge. However, the policemen kept a firm hold of the youth and dragged him to safety. When the young man, John Roach, realised the danger he had been saved from he was apologetic for resisting their help and was extremely grateful to his rescuers.

How Roach had fallen asleep at such a perilous spot was easily explained. He had been minding cows in a field near the cliffs. Feeling tired, he lay down to rest by a nearby hedge and fell asleep. In his slumber he rolled several yards down the slope to the cliff edge. Only luck had prevented him falling over the precipice. One of his arms rested on the inside of a large tuft of bent grass and saved him from rolling any further. The youth was so close to the edge that part of his coat hung over it.

❧❧❧

A rchibald Hamilton Rowan (1751–1834) famously escaped right before his jailers' eyes in a daring getaway. Rowan was a prominent member of the United Irishmen movement and was jailed for two years in 1794 for 'seditious libel' after the movement was outlawed. While he was in Newgate Prison he received visitors and met with Reverend William Jackson, Theobald Wolfe Tone and others to continue to plan their opposition to British rule. Reverend Jackson was betrayed by a British spy, arrested and charged with high treason, which carried the death sentence.

Rowan knew it was only a matter of time before he would also face this charge and decided to escape if he could. A few days later, on 1 May 1794, an escape plan was put in motion. Rowan was able to persuade the prison under-warder, who believed that he had been jailed for political libel, to let him visit his wife on the pretence of signing legal documents. The jailer agreed to his request and escorted the prisoner to his home at 1 Lower Dominick Street, Dublin. They were welcomed by Rowan's wife, who had supper prepared in the front room of the second floor.

After supper Rowan received the jailer's permission to say a word or two in private to his wife in the adjoining room. The jailer consented as long as the door between the rooms remained open, and he shifted his chair at the dining table to watch the doorway. In a few seconds Rowan was beyond his reach, having slipped down a rope that had been slung from the window of the other room. A saddled horse was waiting for him in the stable and Rowan rode away wearing a peasant's rough coat to disguise him. He fled to France, where he was briefly arrested as a British spy. On his release Rowan decided to leave the dangers of revolutionary France and sailed for America.

After a few years he travelled to neutral Germany without being arrested and was reunited with his family there in 1799. In 1806 he was allowed to return to Ireland on the condition that he agreed to be a model citizen.

✤❧❧✤

The Club House Hotel in Kilkenny city, one of Ireland's oldest surviving hotels, was once the headquarters of the Kilkenny Hunt Club. Even after it became a hotel in 1817 it kept a strong link with the club, which retained rooms in the hotel. The hotel was the scene of an extraordinary wager between two members of the club. On 17 February 1857 John Courtney of Ballyredmond, County Cork performed a remarkable feat of horsemanship for a bet with one Charles White.

During supper in the clubroom, Courtney sent for his 'well-known' grey horse White Lion. Mounting it in the hotel hallway, Courtney rode it up two flights of stairs into the clubroom, round the supper table, and after jumping a fire screen, rode White Lion down the stairs again without any accident. His feat greatly impressed witnesses and was talked about for years. The difficult task of riding down stairs was made all the more dangerous by the fact that each stair was bound with thick plates of brass. If one or more of the horse's shod hooves had caught or slipped on them, horse and rider would have fallen down the stairs.

❦❦❦

In front of a large crowd of spectators, Baron Osset of the 16th Lancers performed an unusual feat in the grounds of Lord Charlemont's house at Marino in Dublin on 8 April 1818. One hundred stones were placed a yard apart and a basket was positioned at one end of the line. Baron Osset was to ride to each stone, dismount and pick it up, ride to the basket, dismount again and drop the stone into the basket. He had to mount and dismount two hundred times.

Osset was given an hour to pick up all the stones, but managed to perform the feat in forty-five minutes. Given that horse and master had not practised the challenge, at first most of the betting was against Osset; but when after a few runs the Baron dismounted to scratch his ear with his foot, while the horse stood quietly waiting his master's commands, the betting turned in his favour.

❦❦❦

Kate Shelley (1865–1912) was born near Dunkerrin, County Offaly. The family emigrated to the United States when she was a baby, settling at Honey Creek, near Moingona, Boone County, Iowa. When Kate was twelve her father died, and because her mother was in poor health Kate had to look after the farm and help raise her four siblings. On 6 July 1881 a heavy thunderstorm caused a flash flood at Honey Creek, washing away timbers that supported the railway bridge. The midnight express train from the west was due to cross over the long Des Moines river bridge and shorter Honey Creek bridge on its way to Chicago.

In accordance with railway regulations, a pusher engine was sent from Moingona to test the track as far as Boone and then return to Moingona. At 11 p.m. Kate and her mother heard the engine cross the nearby Des Moines bridge, but as it crossed Honey Creek bridge the weakened structure collapsed. They heard 'the horrible crash and the fierce hissing of steam' as the engine plunged into the swollen waters below. The Chicago train was due within an hour and unless the driver was warned it would suffer the same fate. Someone had to get to Moingona and stop the train. There was no one but Kate to make the journey.

The seventeen-year-old ventured out into the storm in an old coat and hat, and carrying a lantern, and made for the Des Moines bridge. Crossing the bridge on foot even in good weather was not an easy task; the long span had no floor and the ties were a yard apart, leaving gaping spaces with nothing beneath but the raging river. Kate had no choice but to crawl across on her hands and knees by the light of the lantern. Even when the lantern went out, she continued undaunted. When she got across the bridge she ran half a mile to Moingona station to raise the alarm. Kate insisted on returning to Honey Creek with the rescue party to look for survivors of the crash. Amazingly, two men were discovered clinging to the branches of a tree and were hauled to safety. Sadly, the other two men were drowned. The inspiring story of Kate's bravery quickly made her a national heroine.

❧❧❧

Charles Byrne (1761–1783), from Littlebridge, County Tyrone, was one of the tallest Irishmen ever to have lived. While some accounts say he was over eight feet tall, skeletal evidence confirms his height at 7 feet 7 inches. Neither of his parents or any of his relations was unusually tall. At the age of 21 Byrne left home to seek his fortune in London and soon found work as a sideshow attraction.

He was billed as the 'modern living Colossus, or wonderful Irish Giant' and was an instant hit with the curious public. For the large sum of two shillings and sixpence the public could visit Byrne every day (except Sunday) between 11 a.m. and 3 p.m., and 5 p.m. and 8 p.m. For a while the giant Irishman was the talk of the town, but by early 1783 interest in him waned. He still remained on show, but the admission fee was now one shilling. Byrne died on 1 June 1783 at the age of 21.

His death was said to have been from excessive drinking. He may also have had tuberculosis. The theft of his life savings, the considerable sum of £770, from his pockets while he was drinking at a London public house in April 1783 was said to have hastened his decline. The unlucky man was also haunted by the thought that after his death his body might fall into the hands of surgeons eager to dissect it. He left instructions that his corpse should be weighted and buried at sea to prevent this.

After Byrne's demise his friends set about carrying out his wishes. They accordingly placed his body in a specially made coffin, but before they set off to bury him at sea they exhibited the casket to the public for a short spell for the fee of two shillings and sixpence per visitor. He was then supposedly buried at sea on 6 June. Amazingly, this was not the end of Byrne's tale; he was not actually buried at sea. Instead, his worst fears came true and his corpse somehow came into the possession of London's famous surgeon and anatomist Dr John Hunter. One story asserts that Hunter bribed Byrne's friends with the huge sum of £500 to get his hands on the corpse. Another story claims that the surgeon's agents substituted the corpse for paving stones of equal weight while the coffin lay locked up in a barn during the trip to sea. Men had hidden in the barn and made the switch, leaving Byrne's friends none the wiser.

Whatever the true story, Dr Hunter took possession of the corpse and conveyed it to his rooms. Terrified of being

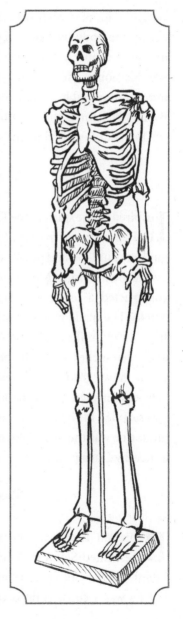

caught and of retribution from Byrne's friends, Hunter cut up the body the same night and boiled the pieces in an immense copper vat until all that was left of the Irish Giant was his bones. He later reassembled the skeleton, but did not put it on public display in his museum for several years. Byrne's skeleton is still on show in the Hunterian Museum at the Royal College of Surgeons in London.

※※※

Inspired by the spirit of the French Revolution, an ingenious United Irishman from Kilrea, County Down built his own guillotine in 1796 and put it aside to use when British rule was overthrown. Samuel Moore, who is described as a 'mechanic', constructed a ten-foot tall guillotine measuring two feet across. The blade was a wide axe weighted with a block cut from an old millstone. It was very sharp and heavy and was about ten inches deep. The blade moved within the wooden frame in two grooves and was raised using a rope and pulley. A few experiments were made on dogs and cats, until Moore was satisfied his invention was in perfect working order. The guillotine was then carefully hidden in the ark of a corn mill at nearby Lisnagrot.

※※※

Benjamin Turner was born in Ireland, but emigrated to the United States with his family when he was only an infant. At the outset of World War I Turner was drafted, but he was a conscientious objector and fled to Mexico to avoid military service. In Mexico City Turner got a job as a bookkeeper for a smelting company and lived there for several years, managing to save several thousand dollars. In 1921 the trusting youth was duped out of a great deal of his savings after falling victim to a confidence scam by notorious conman Ramon Argeiles.

When Turner discovered that Argeiles had swindled him he was furious. He bought a gun, then went looking for vengeance, and after a brief argument he shot and killed Argeiles. Turner was thrown into prison to rot while awaiting trial. With no one to help him Turner despaired, but he was visited by a fellow American citizen who introduced himself as James Hallen. Coincidentally, Hallen had been born in County Clare and, like Turner, had emigrated with his family to the United States as an infant. Turner related his story and Hallen, who was a lawyer, offered to work to get him released – for a fee. Turner gave him a cheque for $1,200 – all the money he had left – and Hallen took it and promptly disappeared.

Luckily for Turner he was later befriended by Constance Kilborne, a kind middle-aged American woman who visited him in prison. She could understand why he had shot Argeiles because she too had been conned out of a large sum of money, by another conman – James Hallen. Constance used her wealth and influence to demand a trial date and hired a lawyer to defend Turner, who had already spent two years in prison. After hearing Turner's story the jury returned a verdict of justified homicide and he was freed immediately.

Just as Monte Cristo sharpened his hate and planned his revenge in prison, so it was with Turner. Years later, Turner described how hatred had kept him alive: 'My hatred was stronger than my despair,' he said. 'I determined then to cling to life so I could follow the man who had taken advantage of my helplessness and left me to die in that unspeakable hole. I would seek out Hallen and shoot him down like the dog he was.' It took him years to save enough to repay Constance Kilborne for her help.

By 1926 Turner was ready to track down Hallen and hired private detectives to locate him. As well as finding out where Hallen lived the detectives discovered that he had an impressive career, dating back to the 1890s, as an international swindler. He had been convicted of grand larceny, forgery, fraud and bigamy and had spent considerable time in jail. He had once been a lawyer, but had been disbarred after his first criminal conviction. Turner traced the conman to his home in the Portland suburb of Falmouth Foreside, where he was living the comfortable life of a retired businessman. On 15 August 1926 Turner showed up on his doorstep and confronted Hallen. They argued and Turner shot him five times, then calmly told terrified eyewitness to get the police while he waited. Before his trial began Turner was quoted in the press as saying, 'Hallen had it coming to him. I'm glad I did it. I will be acquitted.' Indeed, if he had answered differently to questions put to him in court he might have been. The description of his years in a hellish Mexican prison earned the sympathy of all and no one doubted Hallen had cruelly tricked him.

At that point in the trial Turner blew his chances of acquittal when the prosecutor asked, 'If you still had a gun and Mr Hallen were to walk into this very courtroom, what would you do?' Without hesitation Turner replied, 'I'd kill that devil Hallen wherever I met him. I'd kill him over and over, a thousand times. If he were here alive and I had a gun, I'd kill him before the eyes of this very jury.' This truthful, but shocking, admission sealed his fate. Turner was found guilty and sentenced to life imprisonment. After his attempts to get a new trial or a pardon came to nothing, a broken Turner went on hunger strike in June 1931 and died a few weeks later.

Despite his name, Henriques the Englishman was actually an Irish-born pirate called Henry Johnson. Other than the fact that he was born somewhere in the north of Ireland, nothing is known about his background. Johnson commanded a sloop, the *Two Brothers*, which had a crew of ninety, mostly Spaniards, and eighteen guns. Johnson was missing his left hand, but this did not stop him. To fire his gun he balanced it on the stub of his left arm, pulling the trigger with his right hand. He could also wield a sword with his good arm.

His ship ranged around the Caribbean hunting for rich pickings. On 20 March 1730 Johnson attacked the *John and Jane* off Swan Island near Jamaica. It was armed with eight carriage guns and ten swivel guns and had a crew of twenty-five men. Johnson had the reputation of being as bloody and ruthless as any pirate, so the sailors had good reason to put up a strong defence. After fighting off the pirates for five hours the exhausted crew surrendered the ship. Ironically, the pirates had been on the verge of breaking away. When the ship was secured the pirates stripped the crew and prepared to hang them all in pairs, despite previously agreeing to spare their lives if they surrendered. The first pair were about to be executed when Johnson and an English pirate named Echlin interceded on the captives' behalf, threatening to kill any pirate who harmed them.

A pregnant female passenger, Mrs Groves, whose husband had been killed fighting the pirates, had been hiding in the hold, but the pirates found her, drove her up on deck and stripped her. A pirate named Pedro Poleas dragged her into the great cabin and assaulted her. The poor woman's screams brought Johnson to the cabin, and, seeing what was happening, he drew his pistol and threatened to kill any man who attempted the least violence to her.

He made every pirate return everything that belonged to Mrs Groves, and Johnson promised her that he would protect her as long as she remained with him.

With twelve other captives, John Cockburn was put ashore on the coast of Honduras. He later made it back to England and wrote a book about his experiences, describing Johnson as a 'man of great courage and bravery'. The Irish pirate was wanted throughout the Americas, but he was never captured. Indeed, his fate is unrecorded, as is that of Mrs Groves.

❧❧❧

The eighteenth century produced many eccentrics, but it was unusual for one family to produce as many as the Eyre family of Eyrecourt, County Galway.

Lord Eyre resided in a luxurious mansion at the heart of a vast estate and lived in some style with little regard for the cost. The house's windows did not open as the peer had no liking for fresh air. Lord Eyre was proud of the fact that he did not own a book, and he spent his time fishing, hunting and gambling on cock-fighting. He presided at table every day from early afternoon until bedtime, working through a huge amount of food, and always had plenty of claret on hand. One peculiarity of the dining room was a cooked ox that was hung up whole in the room. Diners were expected to help themselves from the carcass.

Lord Eyre was succeeded by his nephew, Colonel Giles Eyre of the Galway Militia, who, presumably due to the lack of books at Eyrecourt, had grown up illiterate. He too led a lavish lifestyle costing some £20,000 a year to maintain. He kept some forty horses and a pack of seventy dogs. Amazingly, Eyre kept a plate of money stacked outside his front door, from which beggars were welcome to help themselves. In 1811 Colonel Eyre stood for parliament for the Galway seat. His opponent was another wealthy Galway landlord, Richard Martin, who cannily offered to withdraw from the election if Eyre would simply sign some meaningless document, but since Eyre could neither read or write he declined the offer. In spite of spending £80,000 on the election Eyre still lost. It was no wonder that by the time he died Eyre had spent his entire fortune.

Giles's cousin, Ned Eyre, was equally wealthy and equally spendthrift. Another cousin, the diarist Dorothea Herbert, had much to say about the foolish but good-humoured wastrel her family doted on. Ned left Galway as a young man and bought a house near Dorothea's home at Carrick-on-Suir. He lived there with his mother, half a dozen servants and two spotted spaniels called Miss Dapper and Miss Kitsey, whom he treated as his daughters and heiresses.

He never came downstairs before noon and lived on tea, cold water and a diet of sweetmeats and pickles of all kinds. Despite this meagre diet Eyre found the energy to get through a £100,000 fortune and died in straitened circumstances while he was abroad avoiding his creditors. Dorothea thought him 'one of the greatest oddities that nature or art ever produced; I say art, because he studied every possible method to make himself different from other human beings.'

Ned dressed strikingly in brightly coloured silks and satins with contrasting linings. He wore satin shoes with jet buckles and 'had two or three sets of paste buttons that cost an immensity. His hair was dressed like a woman's over a rouleau or tete, which was then the fashion among the ladies. He sometimes carried a muff, sometimes a fan, and was always painted to the eyes with the deepest carmine.' Ned was as outrageous as his dress and spent most of his time planning 'some ludicrous exploit or excursion that spared no expense in its execution'.

Dorothea and her sisters accompanied Ned on one such trip to Galway and the Loughrea races. They all set off in Ned's specially designed glass coach with the two dogs and a retinue of servants. On arrival they were greeted by the ringing of the town bells. The first thing Ned did was to open the family vault and view the remains of his great aunt. Such sacrilege did not pass unnoticed. A hostile crowd gathered and he was lucky to escape unharmed. Next Ned invited 'all the beggars of Galway to hot toast, tea, and chocolate' at his lodgings every morning. No one was turned away and all left with a shilling. Another amusement was dressing a servant up as an infant and dandling him on his knee in full view of a nurse and child who lived across the street. Dorothea recalls 'the fine folks of the town soon heard of our doings and came in a body one Sunday to stare and gaze.' Ned soon got rid of the crowd by poking his head out of a window and sticking his tongue out. On the trip to the races Ned loaded his coach with peaches and apricots for the Misses Dapper and Kitsey to enjoy. On the return trip to Waterford Ned loaded the coach with fish, 'which soon stank so abominably that there was no bearing it'. Despite his vast fortune, Ned's extravagances left him in debt most of his life.

In 1610 Lord Cork decided to embark on the ambitious project of constructing a wall around the town of Bandon, County Cork to defend it. An area of some 25 acres was to be enclosed by a wall, nine-foot thick, that varied in height from 30 to 50 feet, complete with six watchtowers. After the work had begun, the stonemasons went on strike. Their wages were twopence halfpenny, but seeing a long job ahead of them, they decided to take advantage of it and demanded three pence a day from Lord Cork. When he refused to pay they marched off, with the exception of one man, who continued to work. Lord Cork, being anxious to complete the walling of the town as quickly as possible, was forced to yield and pay the strikers what they had demanded. When they found their fellow stonemason still working away, the men decided to deal with him before the day was out. During the day they prepared a grave for him in the walls, and, gathering round him when they stopped work in the evening, one of them came behind him and hit him on the head with a pickaxe, killing him instantly.

They then laid him in his tomb, placing the pickaxe and his hammer and trowel beside him, covered him with a large slab and quickly ran a course of masonry over it to hide the grave. The unfortunate man was missed, but nobody found out what had happened to him. Over the course of time the story of the murdered mason bricked up in the walls leaked out and was passed down from one generation to another. Two hundred years later, two labourers were removing part of the old town wall when they found the grave and the skeleton of the murdered mason. When it was exposed to the air it soon crumbled into dust, but the hammer, trowel and pickaxe were in a good state of preservation.

James Levy was born in Dublin in 1842 to Jewish parents and emigrated to the United States with his family as a young boy. He later became a gunslinger in the wild west and was famously involved in one of the most dramatic shootouts ever. Little is known of his early years, but by 1871 Levy was working at silver mines in Pioche, Nevada. On 30 May of that year Levy witnessed two miners fighting. One of them, Mike Casey, shot and fatally wounded Thomas Gosson. At the inquest Casey claimed self-defence, but Levy testified that Casey had fired the first shot. Casey challenged Levy to a gunfight and the Irishman obliged. His first shot grazed Casey's head, the second got him in the neck, but Levy was unhurt.

As the wounded man collapsed, Levy bashed his skull in with his pistol. One of the bystanders, who was a friend of Casey's, pulled out a pistol and shot Levy in the jaw. But the shot came too late to save Casey. Levy lost several teeth, but survived, and was later accused of Casey's murder. After this Levy gave up mining and started travelling the Old West making a living as a professional regulator and gambler. It is estimated that he survived some sixteen shootouts over the next few years. The hardened gunfighter was accused of murder several times, but was never convicted.

The celebrated gunfight that earned him a place in the history of the west took place on 9 March 1877. Levy and another gambler, Charlie Harrison, fell into an argument in Shingle and Locke's saloon in Cheyenne, Wyoming. The argument escalated when Harrison made derogatory remarks about Levy's Jewish–Irish heritage. Levy took offence and challenged Harrison to a gunfight. His opponent was happy to oblige and the two men met in front of Frenchy's saloon on Eddy Street.

The exact details of the encounter are lost to history. We do not know how far apart the duellists stood or who went for his gun first, but it seems that it was the sort of archetypal gunfight familiar to us from films, television and books. Both men drew and fired. Harrison got off the first shots, but he fired wildly and missed the Irishman. Levy, on the other hand, calmly ignored the bullets flying around him, took careful aim and hit Harrison, who fell to the ground. With his pistol aimed at Harrison, Levy walked over to the wounded man and fired another shot into his adversary. Harrison lingered until 22 March before dying of his wound. Levy faced no charges for the killing. Word of the gunfight spread and more famous gunmen, such as Wyatt Earp and Bat Masterson, said the shootout was a perfect example of how it was more important for a shooter to be accurate than fast.

Levy met his end in a suitably violent fashion in Tucson, Arizona on 5 June 1882. He was drinking at the Fashion saloon when he got into an argument with faro dealer John Murphy. After the two agreed to a gunfight, Murphy learned about Levy's reputation and decided to ambush him instead. With two friends, he later waylaid an unarmed Levy and killed him. The men fled and were never caught.

❧❧❧❧

Few people realise that the Doggett's Coat and Badge Race, which is run on the River Thames every year, was founded by an Irishman. Dublin-born Thomas Doggett (*c.* 1640–1721) was a highly regarded actor of his time. His reasons for establishing the race are not known. One story claims that Doggett fell overboard as he was travelling on the river and was rescued by a waterman. (These men performed the vital service of transporting people and goods up and down the river.) Doggett was said to have founded the race in gratitude.

Whatever his inspiration, Doggett officially started the race on 1 August 1715 to commemorate the accession of King George I to the throne one year before. Originally, six apprentice watermen competed for the honour of winning the race over a distance of 4½ miles on the River Thames. The winner's prize was a traditional waterman's red coat with a silver badge attached to the sleeve displaying the white horse of the house of Hanover and the word 'liberty'. The contest was formerly staged on 1 August, against the tide, in the boats used by watermen, but now it takes place in July, with the incoming tide, in modern sculling boats. Although many aspects of the race have changed over the years it remains a prestigious annual fixture. After Doggett's death the Worshipful Company of Fishmongers took over the management of the race and they continue this undertaking to this day.

❧❧❧

When the eccentric 2nd Viscount Mountmorres from County Kilkenny had finished preparing a speech he intended to deliver to the Irish House of Lords he was so pleased with his jottings he handed a copy of it to the press before the debate took place. Mountmorres had anticipated a warm reception for his speech, and had written the words, 'cheering', 'clapping' and 'wild applause', at strategic points in the margin. The debate was postponed, and the speech was never delivered, although it was published in the press.

Lord Mountmorres shot himself in 1797, apparently still deeply troubled by disappointment in love twenty years before. He had paid court to a young lady who had rejected his affections. This did not deter Mountmorres: he learned she was staying at a nearby inn and surprised her at breakfast in an attempt to abduct her. Her cries for help brought her friends and servants and the peer was so savagely beaten that he never fully recovered.

❧❧❧

An equestrian statue of King William III (better known as William of Orange) was unveiled at College Green, Dublin, on 12 July 1701 with great pomp and fanfare. It served as a focal point for celebrations of the Battle of the Boyne and King William's birthday on 4 November. By the 1790s the statue was the centre of celebrations by Orangemen on 12 July and 4 November. On these days the horse was painted white, while the figure of King William was draped with an orange cloak and sash. The horse was garlanded with orange lilies and ribbons. A bunch of green and white ribbons was symbolically placed under the horse's uplifted foot, which enraged nationalist sentiment. Over the years the statue was subject to several acts of vandalism, the most celebrated of which took place in 1805.

With 4 November falling on a Sunday, the celebrations were postponed until the following day. At midnight on 3 November a watchman on duty on College Green was disturbed at his post by a painter, who said he had been sent by the city corporation to prepare the statue for the approaching ceremony, adding that the nationalists' protests had made it wiser to do it at night. Having gained access to the statue the workman set to work. After some time he descended from his ladder and asked the watchman to mind his painting equipment while he went back to his employer's warehouse to get some material needed to complete the decorations. However, the man did not return.

At daybreak on Sunday it was clear why he had not returned. The statue was completely covered with a sticky black paint mixed with tar and grease, which was extremely difficult to remove. Fortunately for the painter he was never found. The statue was finally taken down after it was badly damaged by an explosion in November 1928.

❧☙❧

Armagh-born architect Francis Johnston (1760–1829) was responsible for several important buildings in

Georgian Dublin. He is perhaps best known for building the General Post Office (GPO) on O'Connell Street. One of the smaller projects Johnston was responsible for was the construction of Richmond Tower at the junction of Watling Street and Queen's Bridge in 1812. The tower became the entrance to the Royal Hospital, Kilmainham, from the city side. Richmond Tower had to be moved after the arrival of the railway in 1847. It was dismantled and re-erected, at the railway company's expense, as the western entrance to the Royal Hospital.

When Johnston originally erected the tower the architect had placed his own coat of arms above the gateway arch and had concealed it with a piece of wood painted to match the stonework. He had planned that the coat of arms would be revealed when the wood had rotted away. His prank was discovered when the tower was taken down for removal. The coat of arms of the Royal Hospital was substituted for that of the Johnston family when the Richmond Tower was rebuilt in its current location.

※⊱⊰※

There have been many cases of murderers escaping detection for several years only to be caught by mere chance. The strange story of Bernard McCann from Newtownhamilton, County Armagh is one such case. In 1813 McCann, then a teenager, was working as a baker in Lisburn. One day he went to the Maze races, where he met a friend from the town, a cattle dealer called Owen McAdam, who had a lot of money on him. McAdam was also known to own an unusual watch with four soldiers on the dial, and a sturdy pony that could carry him from Belfast to Dundalk in less than a day. The two men were seen together, drinking heavily, in several public houses that day.

A few days later McAdam's body was found in the River Lagan. The medical evidence showed that he had been murdered, then thrown into the water. There was no sign of his money, watch or pony. The morning after the races McCann went to his employer and told him he had found a better job, then left, taking all his belongings. After the discovery of the corpse a warrant was issued for his arrest, but he was long gone. However, a man fitting his description had sold McAdam's unusual watch and also left the pony with an innkeeper, saying that someone would pick it up.

Ten years later a baker who had known McCann in Lisburn was in Galway city and spotted the wanted man. Although many years had passed and McCann was now a 17-stone man in his mid-twenties, the baker was certain of his identity and reported it to the mayor of Galway. The mayor found it hard to believe that a respected businessman who was known for his charitable deeds and generosity was a murderer. The man known to him as James Hughes was a wealthy butcher in the city, with a wife and five children.

At first the mayor did not credit the accusation, but the stranger's story was so persuasive he ordered the arrest of Hughes and invited him to explain the accusations. It was quickly clear that Hughes, who claimed to be from Dungannon, did not know the names of several people he should have been familiar with. McCann was transferred to Downpatrick gaol and tried for McAdam's murder. He still claimed to be James Hughes, but could produce no witnesses who knew him by that name before 1813. On the other hand, several people swore to his real identity.

The evidence against him was compelling and McCann was found guilty and sentenced to death. The administration of justice did not delay in those days and McCann was executed outside Downpatrick gaol the following day, 29 July 1823. On the scaffold McCann admitted his guilt and sought forgiveness for his crime. His execution by hanging was notable by going badly wrong. When the trap was pulled, McCann fell, but not to his death. Under his weight the rope snapped and he fell twenty feet to the ground. He landed on his feet, but with his arms pinioned, he fell backwards.

Soldiers carried him back inside the prison to wait while a stronger rope was procured. Stunned by the shock of the fall, it took the condemned man a few minutes to recover. He sat upright on his own coffin and asked for a drink of water. McCann remained sitting there for an hour and a half until the hanging could proceed, then he calmly walked to the scaffold, but was more afraid of another fall than his death. This time the execution proceeded smoothly.

❧❧❧

A swarm of bees routed a regiment of soldiers about to seize insurgent leader Bagenal Harvey's Bargy Castle in Wexford in 1798. The soldiers disturbed beehives in the vicinity and the infuriated bees attacked the redcoats, who fled.

❧☙

There are many traditional Irish folk cures for whooping cough, many of them very old. One of the strangest was to pass a sick child under a donkey's belly and over its back three times. One of the earliest recorded instances of this cure being carried out was on 13 October 1835 in Carrier Street, St Giles, London. An Irish couple living there had a child who was seriously ill with whooping cough. They borrowed a donkey from a local fruit and vegetable seller and brought it home, standing it outside their door.

The father brought the child downstairs and stood on one side of the donkey, while the wife was on the other. They passed the child from one to the other over the back and under the belly of the animal three times. Each time this happened the donkey was given a piece of bread to eat. The sick child was then made to kiss the nose of the animal three times, and after saying a short prayer they put the child back in bed. A large group of people gathered to watch this odd ceremony.

❧❧❧

A man was repairing a seventy-foot high chimney shaft at Kynoch's Chemical Works in Arklow, County Wicklow in May 1902 when he missed his footing and fell. In the fall his clothes caught on a huge nail and held him there until help arrived to rescue the dangling man.

❧❧❧

Sometime in April 1815 a young woman was playing with an infant at Aston Quay near O'Connell Bridge in Dublin. Suddenly the child jumped out of her arms and fell into the River Liffey below. The woman screamed for help and spectators watched in horror as the child sank into the water and failed to surface. A Newfoundland dog that had been passing by with its owner 'sprang forward to the wall and gazed wistfully at the ripple in the water, made by the child's descent'. At the same moment the child reappeared on the surface and the dog jumped in to rescue it. The boy sank again, but the dog remained swimming round and round the spot where he had disappeared. When the child rose to the surface again, the dog seized him and swam to the riverside, where both child and dog were helped ashore.

Meanwhile a gentleman arrived on the scene and asked someone in the crowd what had happened. Learning of the dog's heart-warming rescue of the child, he was astounded by its actions. Another shock was in store for the man when he learned it was his own son who had been rescued: 'a mixed sensation of terror, joy, and surprise, struck him mute!' When he had recovered his wits the man hugged and kissed his child and 'lavished a thousand embraces' on the dog. He offered to buy the dog for the incredible sum of £500, but its master refused to sell his beloved pet at any price.

❧❦❧

Alexander Pearce (1790–1824) from Clones, County Monaghan was transported to Tasmania in 1819 for stealing six pairs of shoes. On arrival he was assigned work as a servant to a settler, but was frequently drunk or absent. When Pearce was caught forging a money order he was sent to the newly opened prison settlement of Sarah Island in Macquarie Harbour in a remote part of the island. Along with seven other convicts Pearce made a daring escape on 20 September 1822, stealing a boat and escaping to the mainland.

It was the start of a nightmarish ordeal for the convicts. They were totally unprepared to survive in the unfamiliar mountainous and heavily forested terrain. After several days they ran out of food and could not live off the land. Weak and faced with starvation, the desperate men drew lots to select someone to be killed and eaten by the others. After the unfortunate man had been killed, cooked and eaten, three of the convicts took fright and fled back to Macquarie Harbour, but the remaining five men continued on.

Three more men were killed and eaten, until finally only Pearce and convict named Greenhill remained. Pearce had stayed alive through a mixture of cunning and luck. He had allied himself to a strong faction in the original group, then when it came down to three men, another man had been bitten by a snake and died. Pearce and Greenhill successfully crossed the mountainous countryside to open land, but the supply of food ran out.

It was now a contest of wills between the starving men, who were afraid to sleep lest the other kill them. After a couple of sleepless nights, Greenhill, who had an axe, was first to collapse from exhaustion, and Pearce grabbed the axe and killed him. When he reached the settled districts Pearce was lucky to meet a convict he knew shepherding sheep. This man kept him hidden for several weeks. Pearce later joined two other outlaws, but all three were eventually caught. In all the Monaghan man had been free for 115 days, and struggling in the wilderness for less than half of that time.

In jail Pearce confessed his act of cannibalism to the chaplain, but was not believed. He was sent back to Sarah Island, but escaped again a few months later with another convict named Thomas Cox. Pearce was captured again within a few days. This time the authorities did believe he was a cannibal – Pearce had parts of Cox's body stuffed into his pockets. He had killed him when Cox had confessed that he could not swim as they were about to cross a river. Even stranger, Pearce had killed Cox even though they had food left. The Monaghan cannibal was sentenced to death and hanged at Hobart Jail on 19 July 1824. Pearce's body was dissected for medical purposes and his skull sent to the Academy of National Sciences in Philadelphia. It was later transferred to the University of Pennsylvania Museum of Archaeology and Anthropology, where it remains to this day.

❧❧

In 1734 a gentleman's horse suddenly grabbed a man's arm with its teeth and threw him to the ground, then lay upon him. Despite all efforts the horse could not be coaxed or beaten off the man and it had to be shot. The injured man survived, but with a broken arm. He had apparently gelded the horse some time previously and the horse remembered him and sought vengeance.

❧❧

Little is known of the eccentric character who was Hugh (Hudy) McGuigan from Draperstown, County Derry. By all accounts he was one of the most extraordinary figures Ireland ever produced. After reading *Don Quixote* and other books of knight errantry, McGuigan was inspired to perform extraordinary feats. The celebrated antiquarian John O'Donovan met McGuigan in 1834, when he was undertaking work for the Ordnance Survey, and recorded that McGuigan 'had leaped 30 feet across the River Moyola, ridden a mad bull at the fair of Magherafelt, ridden his horse, Bucephalus over horses and cows standing at the fair of Tobermore without doing the slightest injury'. It is said McGuigan thought he could fly. He made himself two enormous wings from the wings of twenty-four geese and jumped off the precipice of Craignashoke. The wings failed and he broke his legs. He had intended to fly across the Irish Channel and land on Mount Snowdon.

Dublin newspaper proprietor John Magee undertook a novel form of revenge against a judge who had wronged him. In 1789 Magee used his newspapers to make a score of attacks against the corrupt Francis Higgins. John Scott, Lord Clonmel was a close friend of Higgins and presided over a trial for libel of Magee by Higgins. Clonmel had Magee jailed when the poor man could not raise an enormous sum for surety pending the trial.

With a biased judge, Magee's conviction was never in doubt. Pending the passing of sentence, Magee was let out of prison. And the wronged man chose to get even with Lord Clonmel. The peer owned a villa, Temple Hill in Monkstown, County Dublin, which had beautiful gardens and grounds. Magee rented a field next door to his residence and advertised a fête to celebrate the birthday of the Prince of Wales. A mob of several thousand showed up and proceeded to enjoy themselves and drink heavily at the many publicans' tents. There were many frivolous amusements – dancing dogs dressed in barristers' costumes, and ass races in which the jockeys wore wigs and gowns. At the climax of the day a 'Grand Olympic pig-hunt' commenced. Magee let loose several slippery pigs in the direction of Lord Clonmel's residence and announced that if anyone could catch one, they could keep it. With that the drunken crowd set off in pursuit of the pigs through Lord Clonmel's beautiful gardens, destroying hedges and everything in the gardens in the process.

❧❧❧

Mary Butters (1770–1850) from Carrickfergus, County Antrim was known as the 'Carnmoney Witch.' From an early age she practised witchcraft, providing remedies to cure ailments. Her speciality was curing cows that had been bewitched. At the beginning of August 1807 her services were requested by Alexander Montgomery of Carnmoney, who owned a cow whose milk could not be churned to butter; and people who drank the milk vomited. Believing that his cow had been bewitched by some Carrickfergus women, he called in Butters to help.

The witch issued her instructions. Alexander Montgomery and a young man named Carnaghan were sent out to the cow house and ordered to stand at the bewitched cow's head with their waistcoats turned inside out until called back inside. Mary Butters remained inside the house with Montgomery's wife Elizabeth, their son David and an elderly woman called Margaret Lee. Butters ordered the chimney blocked and every crevice carefully sealed.

Then she proceeded to brew a potion in a large pot over the fire using milk from the cow and some iron objects. Hearing no word after several hours, Montgomery went to the house to investigate. Breaking the door down, he found all four people lying on the floor. His wife and son were dead and Mary Butters and Margaret Lee were barely breathing. Lee died a few minutes later, but Butters recovered – despite being thrown on a dung heap and repeatedly kicked by the furious Montgomery.

At the inquest, the jury decided that the deaths had resulted from suffocation by the noxious fumes emitted by the foul brew Mary Butters had prepared to cure the cow. Butters stood trial before the Carrickfergus Spring Assizes in March 1808, but the charges against her were dismissed by proclamation. She continued to practise her arts and local farmers desperate to cure their bewitched cows still resorted to her remedies.

❦❧

Galway-born Richard Kirwan (1733–1812) was an eccentric scholar famous for his studies, particularly in mineralogy, geology and meteorology. He settled at 6 Cavendish Row, Upper O'Connell Street, Dublin for the last thirty years of his life and enjoyed an eccentric lifestyle. Kirwan suffered from dysphagia, which makes it difficult to swallow. Embarrassed by his condition, he always dined alone. His diet consisted solely of milk and ham. The ham was cooked on Sunday and reheated every day for the rest of the week.

Kirwan was also a hypochondriac and went to extreme lengths to avoid catching colds. His living room had a huge fire blazing in it all year round. Before going outside, Kirwan would stand in front of the fire for some time absorbing the heat. He believed that the human body could store heat like a large Thermos flask and always wore a large hat indoors and outdoors. When he did venture outside he would walk very briskly with his mouth shut, so that no body heat would escape, and he refused to talk to anyone for the same reason.

Kirwan lived by himself, attended by a faithful servant called Pope, who slept in the same room as his master; one of his duties was to wake Kirwan up every few hours during the night and pour hot tea down his throat. This nocturnal tea drinking was to maintain Kirwan's body temperature through the night. Sometimes a sleepy Pope poured the tea into Kirwan's eye rather than his mouth. Eccentric as he was, Kirwan was a model landlord and kept a keen interest in his family's estate in Galway.

On walks Kirwan was usually accompanied by several large dogs. He preferred them to small ones because his dogs had once saved his life when he was attacked, while sleeping, by six wild boars. Kirwan also kept a tame eagle, which he had trained himself, and which always sat on his shoulder – until a friend accidentally shot the bird just as it was returning to its master's shoulder.

Despite his eccentricities, Kirwan was not a hermit. He was a popular host and his home was a regular meeting place for friends and acquaintances. Soirées were held on Thursdays and Fridays, always beginning at six and ending at nine o'clock sharp. At seven o'clock Kirwan had the door knocker from the hall door removed and no further guests were admitted. He played the host, reclining on a couch before the fire, wrapped in cloaks and wearing his hat. When the hour came for his guests to leave he would start to make subtle hints, but if that failed he would personally escort his guests to the door. In spite of all his precautions, in June 1812, at the age of 79, Kirwan caught a cold and died. Pope was later buried in the same grave.

❦

Mary Mallon (1869–1938) from Cookstown, County Tyrone is better known as Typhoid Mary. She was a walking typhoid epidemic, the first person identified as a healthy carrier of the deadly pathogens that caused typhoid fever. Between 1900 and 1907 she worked as a cook for several New York families and numerous people came down with typhoid fever.

It was only in 1906, when one family hired a typhoid investigator named George Soper, that Mallon came under suspicion as being the source of the outbreak. When he confronted her with his suspicions she angrily sent Soper packing, but, undaunted, he compiled a five-year history of her employers and discovered that of the eight families Mallon had worked for, members of seven families had contracted typhoid fever. Soper took his findings to the New York City Health Department. They in turn questioned Mary Mallon, and when she refused to co-operate they arrested the cook and took her into custody.

Tests showed that she had a reservoir of typhoid bacteria in her gall bladder, but she refused to have it removed. She was also unwilling to stop working as a cook. Her unyielding stance left the Health Department with few options. They labelled Mary Mallon a disease carrier and kept her in isolation at a hospital on North Brother Island off New York for three years. In 1910 she was offered her freedom on condition she stopped working as a cook. Mallon agreed to the terms and was released from quarantine.

At first she worked as a laundress, but the work did not pay as well as cooking, so she went back to her old occupation. She used a different name and changed jobs frequently to make it impossible for Soper and the authorities to find her. Wherever she worked over the next five years typhoid outbreaks followed. The worst instance was in 1915, when she caused a major outbreak in a New York hospital: twenty-five people were infected and two died. The police tracked her down a short while later and Mallon was quickly returned to quarantine on North Brother Island in March 1915.

Still unwilling to have her gall bladder removed, and refusing to accept her condition, the unfortunate woman was confined to the island for the rest of her days. It is estimated that she was responsible for infecting fifty-four people, of whom three died, but the exact number will never be known.

❧❧❧

William Burke (1792–1829) from Strabane, County Tyrone and William Hare (1792–?)from Poyntzpass, County Armagh are better known as the infamous duo Burke and Hare, who were responsible for a series of murders committed in Edinburgh in 1828.

There were so few cadavers available for studying and teaching anatomy in British medical schools that there was always a demand for fresh corpses; and surgeons did not care where they came from. Medical schools increasingly relied on body snatchers to provide fresh corpses stolen from graves for a fee. When an elderly lodger died of natural causes in Hare's boarding house in November 1827, the pair sold the corpse to Dr Robert Knox for the princely sum of £7 10s. The men were delighted and decided it was worthwhile killing people and selling the corpses to Knox.

Over several months they lured some sixteen people to the boarding house, usually getting their victims drunk and then suffocating them. Eventually Burke and Hare were caught, but the evidence against the pair was far from conclusive. Hare was granted immunity from prosecution if he confessed and testified against Burke. Needless to say, Hare accepted the deal, and Burke was found guilty and hanged in Edinburgh on 28 January 1829 in front of a huge crowd of 25,000 who, despite the terrible weather, turned out to witness the notorious man's execution. Burke was publicly dissected in the anatomy theatre of Edinburgh University. There was a huge demand for tickets and a minor riot was caused when people were refused admittance. Calm was restored when groups of fifty people at a time were allowed to pass through the theatre.

Burke's skeleton is now displayed in the Anatomy Museum of Edinburgh Medical School, and his death mask and a book said to be made from his tanned skin can be seen at Surgeons' Hall Museum. Hare was freed from jail and disappeared. Dr Knox was never prosecuted after Burke swore he had known nothing of the origin of the cadavers.

❧❧❧

In September 1852 an Irishwoman travelled from Liverpool to Manchester by train. Having bought tickets for herself and two children she deposited a large box, four feet by two feet and two feet deep, with the porters. It was packed into a luggage car without any particular care. When the train reached Manchester the woman and her children got off the train and claimed their box, which had been unloaded from the train without ceremony. To the amazement of the porters and railway staff she opened the box and out popped two children, aged about ten or twelve, who had been packed inside like sardines, with their heads at opposite ends of the box.

The children were extremely lucky to have escaped unharmed and without being suffocated as there were no ventilation holes in the box except for a small hole in the lid. The railway company tried to claim for extra tickets from the woman, but were met with laughter. As they could not detain the children the only satisfaction to be got was by retaining the box until a fine of two shillings and 7½ pence was paid.

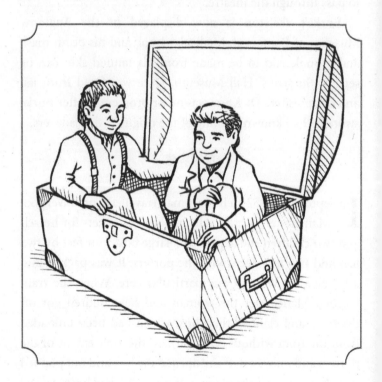

❧❧❧

James Gill, a steeplejack from Newry, County Down, earned notoriety and fame worldwide in 1904 when he evaded capture by the police by climbing up a dangerously unsound seventy-foot chimney and daring them to arrest him. He held out for several weeks before being caught.

Gill had been in an affray with some neighbours and a fight had broken out. He was later arrested for assault and sentenced to a month's jail with hard labour. At the same time Gill had obtained a contract to pull down, for £10, an old and very unsafe chimney at the Sugar Island salt works in Newry. He explained this to the police and asked permission to climb to the top of the chimney, remove a few bricks and establish his claim to the contract, which he would resume when he returned from prison.

Gill was granted this indulgence by the sympathetic police, but once he was safely ensconced at the top of the chimney the cheeky steeplejack laughed down at them and dared the police to come up and get him. The tower was seventy feet high and no more than three or four feet in diameter. The entrance to the chimney was by a small archway at the base through which an ordinary person could crawl through. Inside the chimney the space was cramped and extremely uninviting. Gill had built a number of platforms at regular stages and used a short ladder to climb from one platform to another, pulling it up after him. At the top the resourceful man had built a large platform and erected a small windlass with a rope attached to lower buckets of bricks and haul up provisions.

On the evening of 23 June Gill set off a firework display from the chimney to entertain hundreds of spectators. The event was judged a big success by all except the police. Every now and again Gill sneaked down from the chimney to visit his family and had several close escapes from the police. Eventually he fell from the chimney and was hurt. He was taken to his home and treated. Although the police paid him a visit they decided not to move him to the prison hospital in Dundalk, and the wily steeplejack later limped back to the chimney and reached the safety of its summit.

The police finally caught him a little later when he paid a visit to his home. After his month's imprisonment in Dundalk jail the steeplejack was in demand on the music hall circuit, where he regaled audiences about his time above the law. During World War I Gill served in the Royal Engineers in Salonika, although he was by then over sixty years old. The popular figure died at his home on Lower Water Street in Newry in August 1926.

A curious wager was decided in Cork city one evening in August 1895. A well-built 35-year-old man named Howard bet £5 that he could swallow six dozen raw eggs within a quarter of an hour. In front of a large audience he succeeded in swallowing the 72 uncooked eggs within the time allowed, and won the wager.

❧❧❧

William Kingston's 1874 book *Stories of Animal Sagacity* contains an account of the intelligence of a horse from County Limerick. Some horses were grazing in a field, but broke out through a hedge into a narrow lane. They galloped along the lane at full speed, terrifying a group of children who were gathering wild flowers there. As the horses drew nearer, the children scrambled up the hedge banks to get out of their way, but one little child stumbled, fell and lay crying in the middle of the narrow lane. When the lead horse saw the child it halted, as did the others behind it. Then, lowering its head, it seized the child by its clothes, tenderly lifted it to the side of the lane and laid it on the soft grass. The horse and its companions then continued their gallop through the narrow lane.

❧❧❧

Michael Carmody, a journeyman weaver, was executed in Cork on 3 May 1734 for felony. His fellow journeyman weavers of the city assembled in a large crowd for the execution and dressed the criminal, hangman and gallows in cotton in order to warn against its use. Since the introduction of cheap cottons the wool weaving business had faced severe difficulties due to a lack of demand for its products, and men like Carmody had been reduced to desperate measures.

In his last moments, Carmody, gave an extraordinary speech to the crowd who had assembled to see him hang:

Give ear, O good people, to words of a dying sinner! I confess I have been guilty of many crimes that necessity obliged me to commit; which starving condition I was in, I am well assured was occasioned by the scarcity of money that had proceeded from the great discouragement of our woollen manufactures. Therefore, good Christians, consider, that if you go on to suppress your own goods by wearing such cottons as I am now clothed in, you will bring your country into misery, which will consequently swarm with such unhappy malefactors as your present subject is.

And the blood of every miserable felon that will hang, after this warning from the gallows, will lie at your doors. And if you have any regard for the prayers of an expiring mortal, I beg you will not buy of the hangman the cotton garments that now adorn the gallows, because I can't rest quiet in my grave if I should see the very things worn that brought me to misery, thievery, and this untimely end; all which I pray of the gentry to hinder their children and servants, for their own character's sakes, though they have no tenderness for their country, because none will hereafter wear cottons, but oyster-women, criminals, hucksters, and common hangmen.

❧❧❧❧

When the ship *White Squall*, bound from Melbourne to Sydney in 1851, put into the Kent Islands in the Bass Straits for water, her cables broke and she was washed onto rocks and wrecked. However, all aboard safely made it to nearby Deal Island and survived for seven weeks until they were rescued on 31 July. They were lucky that some of the ship's supplies had been saved, especially since there was one more survivor by the time the crew and passengers reached the island.

Mr and Mrs Richard Keyes from Londonderry had six children in their lifeboat when they left the stranded ship, and seven when they reached the shore, Mrs Keyes having given birth to a baby while in the boat. There was a lighthouse on the island, and a goat belonging to the keeper William Baudinet and his wife Augusta kept the newborn boy fed with milk until the survivors were rescued. The boy was christened Kent in honour of his unusual and dramatic arrival into the world.

❧❧❧❧

John Conway Bourke (1815–1902) from Rathkeale in County Limerick earned a place of honour in Australia's history as Victoria's first overland mailman. The state began an overland mail service on 1 January 1838. Before that the mail went by sea between Melbourne and Sydney, and the service was so erratic that it often took three months to get a reply to a letter. Bourke was to ride the first leg of the journey to Yass. The tough Limerick man collected the mail from the postmaster, packed his saddlebags and set off armed with an old pair of duelling pistols. It took him six days to cross the rugged terrain, and he had several adventures along the way.

One morning Bourke's sixth sense woke him near dawn. He found himself surrounded by a ring of tribesmen sneaking in to attack. Grabbing the mailbag, Bourke leaped for his horse and rode it at full gallop through a volley of spears. He was unhurt, but the horse was slightly injured. Bourke coaxed it on and managed to reach the Murray River. While trying to swim his horse across the animal got stuck in soft clay. Bourke unloaded the saddle and mailbag, but the horse could not budge. There was nothing for it but to swim the river and get help at Howlong.

After a tough swim across the river, Bourke found that he had lost most of his bundle of clothing. He had to set off, almost naked, for nearby Weatherall's station. Bourke later wrote, 'a pack of 50 dogs caught sight of me, and with a common impulse came on like a tornado of devils. There was not much time to think and you can't appeal to a pack of hungry dogs upon the sacredness of the person of Her Majesty's mail.' Bourke saw a large gum tree nearby and climbed up out of their reach. 'Mr Weatherall came along with a gun and calmly proceeded to take aim, with the assurance that if I did not come down in half a jiffy he would blow some of the feathers off me.' Weatherall demanded, 'Who are you, anyway, and what do you want?' Bourke replied, 'I am Her Majesty's mail from Melbourne.' Weatherall sat down and laughed. He looked Bourke over and said, 'So you are the mailman, are you? Well, I don't think much of your uniform.'

Bourke borrowed some clothes and a horse and galloped back to the river for his own horse, but the wounded animal could not be helped and he put it out of its misery. He made Yass in six days, but the mail then went on by bullock team, taking another five weeks to reach Sydney. John Conway Bourke continued riding that route for three years until a mail coach was established in 1841. It was said that Bourke never lost a letter on his journeys. In later years the Limerick man became a publican in Melbourne and died in 1902 at the age of 87.

❧❧❧

Robert Barnewall, Lord Trimblestown was a wealthy landowner of Trimblestown Castle, near Trim, County Meath. As a young man he travelled widely and studied medicine and botany. When his father died in 1746, Lord Trimblestown returned to his ancestral home and made his name as a skilled physician, drawing his clientele from all strata of society. The peer seems to have been particularly skilled at treating nervous ailments, if we can judge from an amusing account of his treatment of a hysterical high society woman. In his 1820 memoirs, Richard Lovell Edgeworth says that the woman had been 'flattered egregiously by one sex, and vehemently envied by the other,' and now, as old age approached and her beauty began to fade, felt that she was 'shrinking into a nobody'. She had consulted many physicians in England and Ireland and was turning to Lord

Trimblestown as a last resort. His method of treatment was certainly unorthodox. The woman was taken into a darkened room lit by green tapers. Four mutes were instructed to swing her vigorously and threaten her with rods. 'By degrees,' we are told, 'the fits of her disorder became less frequent, the ministration of her tormentors less necessary, and in time the habits of hypochondriacism were so often interrupted, and such a new series of ideas was introduced into her mind, that she recovered perfect health, and preserved to the end of her life sincere gratitude for her adventurous physician.'

Lord Trimblestown was well liked and known for his kindness. He treated the poor without charge and often gave out free medicine. As a young boy the actor and writer John O'Keefe stayed at Trimblestown Castle for several weeks while his father was being treated for an illness. The time spent there made a lasting impression on the boy. He was particularly impressed with a large eagle kept chained up by the front door, which the servants fed by throwing it pieces of meat from a safe distance. O'Keefe witnessed the eagle pounce on the back of an unlucky foxhound, who, attracted by the meat, ventured too close and paid for its daring.

❧❧

During the Peninsular War against Napoleon Bonaparte it was decided that an Allied army should land in south-eastern Spain to fight the French on a second front while Wellington's force was in Portugal. The first and second divisions of the 27th Regiment were part of this force, landing in Spain in 1812.

The Battle of Castalla took place on 13 May 1813 when three divisions of the French army tried to dislodge the Allied forces from a commanding position on a high ridge centred on the castle of Castalla. When an attempt to assault one end of the line failed, the French commander gave the order to deploy from column into line formation. While this manoeuvre was taking place an extraordinary encounter occurred. A French grenadier officer stepped forward and challenged 'any English officer' to single combat. Captain John Waldron of the 2nd Inniskillings, 'an agile Irishman of boiling courage', took him up on the challenge and both sides looked on as the officers met each other. The combat did not last long; Waldron quickly cleft the Frenchman's head with his sword. He had just enough time to pick up his opponent's sword before his roaring battalion raced downhill with bayonets fixed and charged the enemy, forcing the French to fall back to a safer position.

The French officer's sword, a sabre d'honneur that had been presented by Napoleon, was sent to the Duke of York, who, aware of Waldron's heroism in previous engagements, promoted him to major.

❦❦

True courage, it seems, knows no danger. In July 1818, a mason and a labourer argued while building the spire of the new Anglican Church in Newry. A boxing match ensued on the scaffolding around the summit of the unfinished building, where the area enclosed by railings was no more than six feet by six feet. Here the combatants fought each other 176 feet above ground. Although they exchanged heavy blows, fortunately neither of the men was 'thrown out of the ring'. The outcome of the fight is not recorded.

At about 2 a.m. on 15 June 1820, a watchman on duty in College Green, Dublin was alerted by a noise coming from inside nearby Home's arcade. Shortly afterwards he saw a figure appear at one of the windows. The watchman, with the help of two men who were passing by, caught a thief inside the premises. He had got into the building through a window, but had not been able to rob any of the shops in the arcade because they were firmly locked. He did manage to steal money from the watchman stationed in the arcade, and also stripped him of his waistcoat and trousers while he was asleep!

❦❦❦

Horace de Vere Cole (1881–1936) from Ballincurrig, County Cork was a notorious hoaxer. His most famous exploit took place on 7 February 1910, when Cole and five friends tricked the British Navy into believing that they were the Prince of Abyssinia and his entourage. Four of them (including the writer Virginia Woolf) stained their faces, necks and hands, pasted on fake beards and dressed up 'Arab-like' in silk robes and jewelled turbans. Cole and another friend wore suits and top hats to play their role as diplomatic officials. Pretending to be from the Foreign Office, Cole sent a telegram to the Admiralty informing them that Prince Makakalen of Abyssinia and his party wished to visit HMS *Dreadnought* that day. He spared no expense and hired a special train at Paddington Station to take the royal party to Weymouth. The party arrived to find a guard of honour waiting, and the VIPs were given the grand tour of England's great warship. No one suspected a thing. Cole told the press about it a few days later, making a laughing stock of the Royal Navy.

The wealthy Cork man carried out several other hoaxes, on one occasion challenging a friend, a newly elected member of parliament, to a race on a London street. Cole secretly slipped his gold watch into the MP's pocket and gave his friend a head start. As soon as his friend started running,

Cole shouted 'Stop, thief!' and a policeman promptly caught the MP. Cole continued the charade that the runner had stolen his watch, leaving his friend speechless. Eventually Cole admitted it was a joke and the men were allowed to go on their way. Unfortunately, Cole began waving his stick around as if he were conducting an imaginary band, at which both men were arrested and taken into custody. While the MP was freed without charge, Cole was found guilty of a breach of the peace and fined.

In 1919, when Cole was in Venice on his honeymoon, he arranged for a pile of horse manure to be shipped in, and one night dumped piles of it in the Piazza San Marco. Given that the city had no horses and could only be reached by boat, the locals were understandably puzzled. It's little wonder that the eccentric prankster frittered away his entire fortune and died in poverty.

❧❧❧

Before the outbreak of World War II, one of the most remarkable residents of the Mackay district in Queensland was 86-year-old Pat O'Mara, whose beard was nine feet three inches long. O'Mara started growing the beard at the age of 22 and never cut it. The beard was in rope form, several inches thick at the top, and tapering a little below the neck to a whip-like form. For the sake of convenience, he wore it coiled up in a linen bag tucked under his shirt. O'Mara was fond of swimming and could often be seen in the water with his beard floating about him like the arms of a strange octopus. O'Mara was born in County Tipperary in 1852 and emigrated to Australia as a young man. He worked as a coach-builder and wheelwright and settled in Townsville, marrying and raising a family. On a number of occasions the hirsute Tipperary man was approached by showmen with attractive offers to go on tour, but he always refused to exhibit his extraordinary beard.

⁂

In August 1816 a poor Dublin man was complaining that he did not have a halfpenny to pay the toll for using the footbridge opposite Church Street. A young man of about sixteen or seventeen years old heard the man, but only having a halfpenny to pay for himself asked the toll collector if a person carrying a load over the bridge paid more than a person with none. When the reply was no, the youth gave the poor man a piggyback ride over the bridge.

⁂

One of the greatest natural disasters ever to hit Ireland occurred on the night of 6 January 1839, when the country was devastated by such a ferocious storm that it came to be known as 'The Night of the Big Wind'. The damage it caused across the land was terrible and several hundred people lost their lives. About 1 a.m. a small house in Ballyshannon, County Donegal, owned by Betty Dunbar, was discovered to be on fire. The owner left it and found shelter at a neighbour's house, but an old pensioner who lodged in the house would not stir, saying that 'he was at too many battles to be frightened by a blast of wind'. With the greatest difficulty the old man was finally persuaded to leave the house. But when he got into the street and saw the flames, he exclaimed 'Well, I have heard of the burning of Moscow, was at the battle of Badajoz, but dang me if this does not beat them hollow!' He then attempted to rush back into the house for his jacket, which contained a Waterloo medal, but the roof falling stopped him in his tracks.

❦❧

While the landlord of an estate at Killakee, County Dublin was absent from his land in January 1820, a poacher named Cavanagh took the opportunity to try his hand at a rabbit warren. Cavanagh set his nets around the warren and sent in his favourite ferret to frighten the rabbits out. The ferret made his way around the burrow for some time before making an exit out of a different hole. A passing eagle pounced on the ferret, caught him in his talons and soared aloft. The poacher was heartbroken at the terrible fate of his 'best friend' and means of support. He decided to go to Dublin, and on reaching Firhouse village, about five miles into his journey, he met a tailor running along the road, crying out that the prophecies of Mother Shipton had come true. One of the eagles mentioned in the prophecies had fallen from the sky, 'accompanied by a hairy demon', and were lying in his potato garden. The crazed man further assured the crowd of people who were gathering around him that 'all nature would be soon at a stand, and a total conflagration of the earth would immediately ensue'. Hearing the man's foolish outburst, Cavanagh continued on, cursing all eagles, but curiosity prompted him to look into the tailor's garden as he passed. There, to his 'surprise and great joy', he found the eagle sprawled on the ground with its windpipe torn asunder, and his pet ferret, twined around its neck, alive and well.

❧❧❧

A gentleman's house on Baggot Street in Dublin was robbed of several items of clothing in July 1818. As the family's servants were beyond suspicion, the theft remained a mystery until a few days later, when the following letter was delivered by penny post:

> Sir – I am a man who lives by robbing – you left your door open on Sunday last, when you thought you shut it, for which you have lost your coat and other articles. I wanted them sadly, for I was bleached with the sun. I could have taken law books, but I am rogue enough without them. Yours truly Pat. Watch-The-Doors.

❧❧❧

Two Irish bricklayer labourers were working on a house near Russell Square in London in September 1805 when one of them boasted he could steadily carry any load to any height. His friend bet he could not carry him on his hod up a ladder to the top of the building they were working on.

This man placed himself on the hod and the friend, after 'a great deal of care and exertion' succeeded in carrying him up and down safely. The man who had been carried paid over the money, agreeing that he had lost, but added, 'Don't you remember? About the third storey you made a slip. I was in hopes.'

❦

During a thunderstorm on 13 May 1911 a remarkable incident occurred at the Malone Golf Club in Belfast, when a golf ball was struck by lightning while in the hands of a player. Jack McMurray was playing a friendly round with Jack McCammond. When the thunder and rain began they made their way to a small shelter. McCammond, who was sitting near the door, took out a knife and began to cut into a golf ball. Suddenly there was a blinding flash of lightning and it struck McCammond's knife and the ball in his hand. His fingers were slightly burned, while the blade was melted and the ball reduced to a putty-like mass.

❦

The 1897 edition of the *Badminton* magazine contains an article by English sportsman A.B. Whittington concerning his annual holidays in County Mayo. For several years Whittington rented the sporting rights of a large estate near Clew Bay. For the modest sum of £2 10s a week Whittington and his friends and family had 10,000 acres, which included five lakes full of trout and numerous rabbit warrens, where they could shoot and fish to their hearts' content. Included was a large furnished mansion sited on a dramatic promontory overlooking the Atlantic Ocean. Whittington loved his time there and the locals loved to see him too. The article lists several roguish ways in which they tried to part him from his money. Whittington wanted to buy a few sheep to have to eat during his stay. Next morning twenty-five would-be vendors appeared, each leading a sheep. Whittington had the sheep lined up and passed his hand over them. He picked out four fat sheep and negotiated a price with the owners, then put the animals out to grass. Next morning the Englishman had a terrible shock. His fine fat sheep 'were all as flat as newspapers', and he could nearly see through them. The wily vendors had filled them up with gallons of water to make them seem fat.

On another occasion Whittington shot a tame goose flying overhead and offered half a crown in compensation to the owner instead of the usual eighteen pence. News spread like wildfire that he was offering a huge bounty. Whittington soon discovered that he had shot nine geese – at least that was the number of claimants holding a dead goose outside his door the next morning. One man had even cut the head off his. Whittington was able to recognise his goose and make a just reward to the owner of his victim.

Whittington was, however, able to get his own back on the locals. After a terrible storm one night he took a walk on the beach and found a recently dead pig that had washed off some passing vessel. Whittington had long warned the locals that he would shoot any pig found on the grounds of his house and not pay any compensation for it. The discovery of the dead pig struck him as a good way of showing his determination. He dragged the pig up the shore and covered it with seaweed to hide it. That night he took the pig towards the house, laid it on the lawn and shot it in the head. Next morning Whittington's local servant and wife, the latter in tears, gave out to him for the terrible thing he had done, murdering a pig belonging to a local widow woman, who would be grief-stricken when she found out. Whittington pretended to be furious, swearing that he was only sorry he hadn't killed more. In due course the poor woman and several friends arrived at the house crying over the loss of the pig. She gave a wonderful performance – Whittington thought she had even put on mourning dress for the occasion – and looked for a sum of several pounds in compensation for her beloved pig. Whittington kept a poker face and laughed at their demands to pay a fair and reasonable sum. Then he led the crowd on, asking what the value of the pig was. After listening to their wild valuations he said he would consider the matter. He kept them waiting for several days before sending for his servant, who was in on the woman's plot. Whittington revealed his ruse and threatened to inform the local magistrate of the attempt to extort money from him. The servant was badly shaken by this and he and his wife got down on their knees and begged for mercy. Whittington let the matter rest, and was never troubled during the rest of his stay.

❧❧❧

L ough Neagh has only been frozen on a handful of occasions during the past few centuries. For several weeks in January 1814 the temperature fell so low that the lake was frozen over from shore to shore. The ice was so thick that one Colonel Langford Rowley Heyland bravely rode from Crumlin Waterfoot to Ram's Island, a distance of nearly a mile and three-quarters. Around the same time a drag race was run around the island by local landowner Stafford Whittle and his pack of harriers. Crowds followed the novel chase. Colonel Heyland had in 1804 ridden around Lough Neagh for a considerable wager. The distance was 63 miles and Heyland performed the feat in a few minutes less than six hours, using fresh horses stationed at regular distances apart.

❧❧❧

D ublin-born Trooper Patrick Fowler (1874–1964) spent most of World War I hiding in a cupboard. Fowler was a member of a British cavalry regiment, the 11th Hussars. On 26 August 1914, Fowler took part in the Battle of Le Cateau, but was cut off from his regiment during a German advance. For five months, Fowler survived in the woods until he was discovered by a local man, Louis Basquin, in January 1915. The Frenchman took pity on the sorry-looking, unshaven, unkempt and half-starved soldier and gave him his lunch. Neither could speak the other's language very well, but

Fowler did not take long to realise that Basquin was prepared to help him. Later that night he led the Irishman to the house of his mother-in-law, Madame Belmont-Gobert, in in the village of Bertry. This woman and her daughter Angèle immediately agreed to hide him in what was now German-occupied territory. As the Germans periodically searched all the houses in the village, they had to find a hiding place for Fowler, and they settled on a cupboard that stood in the kitchen. It was five feet six inches tall and twenty inches deep with a vertical wooden partition dividing it into two sections. When Fowler squeezed into one side of the cupboard, little did he think it would be his home for almost four years. Neither could he have foreseen the anxious days and nights of sleepless torture he would endure with his knees hunched up to his chin, not daring to move or scarcely breathe, terrified that he might cough or sneeze, or that the Germans would see through Mme Belmont-Gobert's clever subterfuge and search the cupboard – although she always left one door of the cupboard open to allay suspicions.

When he first entered his tiny refuge Fowler thought he would only be there for a few days until he could be smuggled across German lines into Holland and get back to England to re-join his regiment. But the Germans dug in and there was little prospect of getting through their lines. Two weeks after Fowler's arrival, sixteen German soldiers were billeted in Mme Belmont-Gobert's farmhouse. They occupied the upper part of the house, but spent most of their time in the kitchen, where Fowler was hidden. He had to remain completely still and silent for hours on end while they were in the room. Fowler was only able to come out of his hiding place late at night to stretch his arms and legs and share the tiny amount of food the family had to live on. Whenever attention turned to the cupboard, Mme Belmont-Gobert diverted the German soldiers by taking down a picture of her other pretty daughter from the mantelpiece and showing it to them.

As the war went on food rationing became more severe. Some of Mme Belmont-Gobert's friends were let into her secret and helped out with scarce food supplies to supplement their rations. Fowler was sometimes so hungry that he stole out from his hiding place and hacked off a few slices of the Germans' unpalatable, though sustaining, black bread. Fowler's health was already poor from the months he had spent outdoors before he came to Bertry, and it was not helped by the conditions he endured in the cupboard. When he fell ill he was treated by a kindly local chemist, who often sent him medicine and other comforts. When another British soldier hiding in the village was betrayed to the Germans and shot, Fowler deemed it too risky to remain in the house any longer; there were bound to be intensive searches for other hidden soldiers. He was fearful for his hosts, too; the family who had looked after the other soldier were jailed for 21 years in Germany.

Dressed as a woman, with an umbrella covering his face, Fowler was led to a nearby barn and hid under it for a month. It was a horrible rat-infested hell-hole, but he bravely endured it until the Germans stopped searching. At night Basquin would creep over and bring him food. When it was safe, Fowler returned to the cupboard. Again dressed as a woman, with a shawl covering his unkempt beard, Fowler was escorted back to the house by Mme Belmont-Gobert.

On the return journey they passed a drunken German. Fowler accidentally let the shawl slip, but Mme Belmont-Gobert saved the day by offering the German a drink from a small bottle of liquor she had, while Fowler covered his face and quickly walked on. A moment later he was joined by his quick-witted French saviour. It was not the only time Fowler disguised himself as a woman; when rumours of another house-to-house search reached Mme Belmont-Gobert, Fowler was hurried outside in his dress and shawl to hide under a haystack. After a few hours buried under the hay Fowler heard German voices. They were looking for a large number of bottles of wine, which they suspected were hidden in the hay. The next thing he knew, the stack was being stabbed by pitchforks; but yet again Fowler's luck held out, and although the forks came perilously close he escaped unhurt.

Months later the Germans requisitioned the entire house for billeting troops and the family had to move to a small cottage some distance away. Along with the rest of their furniture the cupboard would have to be moved to the cottage. It was decided that Fowler remain inside while it was moved. Basquin and a trusted friend were called in to move the cupboard. As they carried it to a waiting cart a passing German lent a hand, also volunteering to unload the cupboard and carry it in to the cottage. It was only after the soldier departed that Fowler was able to breathe a sigh of relief. The cupboard was only ever searched once, and by a stroke of luck Fowler was not inside it at the time. One evening he had been relaxing in an armchair enjoying the company of Mme Belmont-Gobert and Angèle when German soldiers knocked at the door. While Angèle fumbled with the door, stalling for time, Fowler sprang back into the cupboard, but before he could pull the door shut Mme Belmont-Gobert gestured to him to hide underneath the mattress of a large feather bed in the room next door. Mme Belmont-Gobert later claimed that she had had a premonition that the cupboard would be searched. Fowler had more freedom in the cottage than before, but he still had to hide in the cupboard when the Germans approached and at night.

Life continued in this way for two more years until the Germans retreated from Bertry on 10 October 1918. When the British forces entered the village Fowler was delighted and went out to meet them. Instead of being greeted as an incredible survivor Fowler was arrested as a deserter and marched back to the British headquarters by two military policemen. Along the way, the men encountered Fowler's former commanding officer and he was released after this man testified to his identity. After the war Fowler settled with his wife and family in Scotland.

Mme Belmont-Gobert, who took such risks to save Patrick Fowler, was awarded the Order of the British Empire for her bravery. When in 1927 she was discovered to be living in poverty, the *Daily Telegraph* launched a campaign to help her. The 11th Hussars presented her with £100 and then gave her full billeting pay for looking after Fowler backdated to 1914. The French government also awarded the heroic woman a pension. The cupboard in which Fowler spent most of the war is now on display in the 11th Hussars' regimental museum in Winchester.

❧❧❧

Lord Charles Beresford (1846–1919) from Curraghmore, County Waterford entered the Royal Navy as a cadet and later rose to the rank of admiral. As a young man he was famous for his escapades and pranks. He once rode a pig down Park Lane in London. This episode happened when Beresford was returning home with a friend early one summer morning. A herd of pigs was being driven by when Beresford spotted a huge animal that stood out from the rest. On the spot he bet his friend £5 that he would ride the giant pig into Piccadilly. Beresford dashed into the herd and took a flying leap on to the pig's back. They galloped all the way down Park Lane, followed by the angry swineherd. 'As I turned into Piccadilly,' Beresford later triumphantly recalled, 'the swineherd caught me a clout on the head, knocking me off my steed. But not before I won my wager.'

On another occasion Beresford was tricked into swimming across the River Thames dressed in a frock coat and top hat. Beresford was at Maidenhead when a fellow scamp named Doddy Johnson challenged him to a swimming race across the Thames, with both men wearing frock coats and top hats, for a wager of £5. The first to reach the other shore was the winner. Both men would run from the same point and jump into the river to swim across. When the starting signal went Beresford raced down the lawn and plunged in. About halfway across the river he looked back and saw Johnson standing on the river bank laughing at him. Beresford continued on and claimed his £5.

Horse-drawn vehicles were banned from using Rotten Row in London's Hyde Park as it was for the use of horse riders only. Beresford bet some friends that he would drive a vehicle on it. At the appointed time his friends gathered to watch the event. While they were waiting a man driving the park water cart came by, and drenched them with water. It was Beresford. He had bribed the water cart driver to take his place so that he could win the bet.